Teaching English to Students from China

T0083658

Edited by

Lee Gek Ling, Laina Ho, J.E. Lisa Meyer
Chitra Varaprasad & Carissa Young

Centre for English Language Communication
National University of Singapore

NUS PRESS
SINGAPORE

Published by:

NUS Press
National University of Singapore
AS3-01-02, 3 Arts Link
Singapore 117569

Fax: (65) 6774-0652
E-mail: nusbooks@nus.edu.sg
Website: http://nuspress.nus.edu.sg

Reprint 2013
Reprint 2019

ISBN 978-9971-69-263-6 (Paper)

The first edition was published by Singapore University Press in 2003.

Typeset by: Scientifik Graphics (Singapore) Pte Ltd
Printed by: Markono Print Media Pte Ltd

Teaching English to Students from China

To our students past, present and future whom we teach and from whom we learn

Contents

Foreword

Teaching English to Students from China is a collection of research articles arising from the Centre of English Language Communication's work in teaching English to students from the People's Republic of China (PRC). Over the last 10 years we have taught over six thousand pre-matriculated students, undergraduates, postgraduates and academic staff members from the PRC in various courses. We have taught them intensive English, English for research, English for academic purposes, business English, engineering English, scientific English and even at one time, legal English. In 1998 Lee Gek Ling suggested that we should publish a book of our pedagogic findings. This idea was well received by our staff and the resulting volume is a reflection of their dedication to providing the most effective teaching methods to our students, as well as their on-going interest in research in English language teaching methodology.

Although our staff members have published their articles in journals and other academic books, this is the first time that we have published a collection of our articles in one volume. May I take this opportunity to commend the contributors for their cooperation and dedication; and also to thank the CELC editorial team for their labours in preparing the manuscript for the Singapore University Press, and also Lena Qua of SUP for her final editing. I thank the Press, now headed by Peter Schoppert, for their foresight in recognising the international application of effective English teaching methods to PRC students.

The underlying rationale was that we would record some of our work in a book, and also share our findings with the wider audience of other such English language teachers. There are many programmes in Australia, Canada, Great Britain and the United States, where increasing numbers of students from the PRC are being prepared for, or taught English on their college and university courses. We look forward to launching this book at the AILA conference to be held in Singapore in December 2002. We hope our work will be useful to others and we also look forward to learning from the research of our international counterparts.

Dr Wong Lian Aik
Director, Centre for English Language Communication
National University of Singapore, 2002

Acknowledgements

Teaching English to our Chinese students is the result of a concerted effort by a team of dedicated teachers.

We would like to thank the Director of CELC — Dr Wong Lian Aik — for his Foreword and his encouraging support of this project. We would also like to record our heartfelt thanks to Ms Thanmoli a/p Peariasamy — our indispensable *Moli* — for reformatting the files and preparing the manuscript.

We also thank Mr Peter Schoppert of SUP for taking us on, as well as Ms Lena Qua for scrutinising the manuscript. We think SUP is farsighted in recognising the growing importance of ELT methodology for foreign students as the number of such students increase. Finally, we are very grateful to the unnamed reviewer who took such an interest in our drafts and who made many valuable comments.

Introduction

English is spoken by over one billion people who have learned it as a foreign language. About 235 million have learned the language as a second language and 337 million speak the language natively (Crystal, 1997: 60–61). Among the one billion foreign language learners of English, a majority come from the People's Republic of China (Kachru, 1982: 356). This huge learner population of Chinese has made the task of successful English teaching in and outside of China all the more important and challenging.

While Chinese learners of English may go through similar language developmental sequences and acquisition orders as learners from other language backgrounds owing to an innate language-specific endowment, it is also indisputable that learners' first language (L1) and cultural background may affect the speed at which learners learn their second language (L2) and pose certain L1-based difficulties to learners in their L2 learning process. The contrastive analysis hypothesis, for example, asserts that where the learner's L1 and L2 are similar, positive transfer would occur to facilitate learners' learning process; where the two languages are different, negative transfer or interference would result to hinder this process (Larsen-Freeman and Long, 1991: 53). Although research has shown that the learning process of second language learners is not as straightforward as stated in the previous sentence, this hypothesis does explain to a certain extent why some interlanguage features, both spoken and written, can be associated with learners of certain L1 backgrounds. For instance, many Chinese learners of English are found to add a schwa /ə/ to word-final consonants, especially plosives, because words in many Chinese dialects take the form of monosyllabic /CV/ or /V/ structure and do not allow consonants in the word-final position (except for the alveolar and velar nasals /n/ and /ŋ/). The confusion of /l/ and /r/, on the other hand, is often associated with Japanese learners of English as the two sounds are free variants in Japanese.

Differences between second language learners with different L1 backgrounds may go beyond linguistic structures and exist at pragmatic, rhetorical, and cultural levels as well. When Japanese learners of

English perform the speech act of refusal in English, for instance, it has been found that the Japanese learners vary their selection of refusal strategies in English according to the refuser's relative status, just as they would do in their native Japanese (Kasper, 1992). On the other hand, in replying to compliments, Chinese learners of English tend to deny the compliment they receive much more frequently than native English speakers do because this is the appropriate way to show their modesty and politeness in Chinese (Golembeski and Yuan, 1995).

Differences in rhetorical structures exist in different languages and cultures as well. For example, Kirkpatrick (1991) finds that Mandarin and English speakers sequence information in different ways in their requests because they have different cultural perceptions about politeness. That is, while English speakers tend to state a request first and give the reasons later, Mandarin speakers prefer to preface a request with some face work, such as with a salutation and reasons. Such differences in rhetoric and culture may lead to breakdowns in cross-cultural communication if not attended to properly.

The existence of such differences at different levels across languages and cultures and the possibility of identifying L1-based interlanguage features in some ways make it easier and more effective to teach a homogeneous learner group. Language educators can design customised teaching materials to cater to the common needs of that particular learner group. Classroom research on such homogeneous learner groups can also generate knowledge about learners of a particular language background to further enhance our understanding of the learners which would, in turn, help improve teaching materials and methodology.

The Centre for English Language Communication (CELC) of the National University of Singapore (NUS) is privileged to have had opportunities to provide an intensive English training programme to a homogeneous learner group from the People's Republic of China since 1992, with about 100–190 students each year. These students, all from about 17 to 20 years of age, have finished their 3-year senior middle school (hence SM3) education and have studied in a university in China for about 3 months. They are then selected by the Ministry of Education of Singapore to come to study at either the National University of Singapore or the Nanyang Technological University on government scholarships. The 6-month intensive English programme (usually from December to June) at CELC happens prior to the students' entry to a university to prepare them for their forthcoming university education in English.

The SM3 students come from different parts of China. They have learned English for about six years in an EFL setting in their home country before coming to Singapore, where English is one of the four official languages and is the language of administration and education. Their English proficiency upon arrival is low intermediate and is roughly the equivalent of that of first year secondary school students in Singapore. The primary aims of the intensive English course at CELC are to improve the students' four basic skills of speaking, listening, reading, and writing, to develop their communicative competence for academic purposes, and to raise their English proficiency from secondary one to secondary four over a period of six months.

As these PRC students have learned their basic English in an EFL setting where teaching is mostly examination-oriented through an intensive reading model, which is the Chinese version of the traditional grammar-translation model (see Larsen-Freeman, 1986; and Feng, this volume), many of them tend to be strong in grammar but very weak in listening and speaking and in writing continuous prose. Their active vocabulary is also very limited. This unbalanced linguistic profile of the students and the challenging task of raising their English proficiency level drastically over a short period of time call for innovative and customised teaching materials and methods.

The eleven chapters in this book represent some of the CELC teachers' attempts to either understand the PRC students' learning habits and strategies or to explore different teaching methods to train these students in a more effective way. The learners in the studies reported here are all from China and are either students in the SM3 intensive English courses at CELC or are postgraduate students at NUS.

In Chapter 1, Feng gives a comprehensive introduction to the ELT situation in China. He traces the history and implementation of the College English Syllabus throughout the country and discusses the impact of this syllabus on the English language teaching method and the kind of student such a teaching mode may create. As the chief aim of the College English Syllabus is "to develop in students strong reading skills so as to enable them to acquire information in their own fields of specialisation" (Feng, this volume: 5), a majority of language teaching practitioners in China have adopted a teacher-centred intensive reading model wherein a written text is dissected and analysed word by word and sentence by sentence to help students understand word meanings and grammatical structures. Although a few people have experimented with the communicative approach in China, this is only a minority and the degree of success seems minimal. As a result, the speaking and listening skills of these PRC learners of English remain rather low.

By asking the students to reflect on their learning processes in their guided diaries, Young and Fong in the second chapter discuss the use of student diaries to record the PRC students' metacognitive awareness and its development over a period of six months. As a result, the authors are able to obtain insights into students' thoughts about their learning, the difficulties they encounter, their learning plans for the future, and even some affective factors such as shyness and interest that may determine how successful a learner can be. They believe that learner diaries can be beneficial to both the teacher and the learner and that positive feedback from the teacher on the diaries can help students tremendously through difficult times.

Chapter 3 by Teng is another report on the use of learner diaries with the PRC students. It differs from Chapter 2 in that the author chooses to use free diaries as compared to the guided diary format used by Young and Fong in Chapter 2. Teng's analysis focuses on the content of the diaries and how such content helps her better understand her students, which, in turn, helps her teach more effectively. For example, through the diaries, Teng is able to identify some specific language difficulties her PRC students have (such as the confusion between 'wish' and 'hope' and 'come' and 'go'), their learning strategies, their subjective beliefs and perceptions about language learning and future needs for university studies, as well as their reactions to classroom activities. The open nature of free diaries also enables the students to reveal some affective elements in their diaries that may help the teacher better understand their difficulties, learning habits and attitudes. General feedback from the PRC students regarding diary writing is positive and the author believes that a learner diary not only provides an effective channel for the teacher to get to know her students, it also offers an opportunity for the students to improve their writing abilities.

In Chapter 4, Goh and Tan use learner diaries through email to examine the similarities and differences between PRC students and Singaporean students in their language learning experiences. They find that the two groups of students differ in the areas of difficulties and motivation levels but are similar in their learning strategies. Specifically, the PRC students tend to have difficulties in speaking, listening, and vocabulary whereas the Singaporean students have trouble with grammar. The PRC students are also more motivated than the Singaporean students. Interestingly, both groups are willing to learn from both the teacher and their peer students and both like group learning. However, Goh and Tan also observe that both the PRC and the Singaporean students use metacognitive strategies inadequately and suggest that teachers help the students identify their specific needs and provide guidance in using learning strategies appropriately.

In her study on PRC students' attitudes towards group work tasks reported in Chapter 5, Meyer uncovers some unexpected tendencies contrary to stereotypes of Asians and Chinese students. That is, the PRC students do not object to group work tasks and peer feedback and do not prioritise group harmony over confrontation. The first two findings coincide with what Goh and Tan observe in their study reported in Chapter 4 — their PRC and Singapore students also favour group learning and are willing to learn from their peers. Meyer suggests that this might be because the PRC students have had some exposure to the outside world through different channels and are therefore open enough to try out classroom activities that may differ from what they have been taught to follow. From a pedagogical perspective, Meyer's findings show that teachers should not refrain from using teaching methods that are new to the PRC students. The vast body of literature on language teaching based on Western student populations may also be applicable to the PRC students as they are receptive to new approaches.

In Chapter 6, Young examines PRC students' attitudes towards Singapore English and whether such attitudes change over time. She finds that these students are rather negative towards Singapore colloquial English at the beginning of their stay in the new country probably because of the difficulties Singapore colloquial English poses to these students, their lack of knowledge about this variety of English, and their lack of communicative competence as a result of the intensive reading teaching they have just gone through. As the length of stay in Singapore increases, however, the PRC students' attitudes towards Singapore colloquial English become more positive. To prevent future PRC students from going through the same learning curve, Young recommends that English teachers in China introduce different varieties of English to their students and that English teachers in Singapore take a more active role in designing materials and activities both in and outside the classroom to familiarise their PRC students with Singapore English.

Chew reflects on the use of the oral strip story technique in her English classes in Chapter 7. Chew modifies the original oral 'Strip Story' format and turns it into a game-like activity so as to add fun to the task and enhance participation. Chew believes that such activities not only create authentic communication situations for students to practise their speaking, listening, vocabulary, and pronunciation, but also give the teacher an opportunity to correct students' production errors in grammar and sentence structure, and promote students' creative thinking and writing abilities. The survey Chew carries out afterwards generally supports her earlier observations and the PRC students are positive about such activities. Most importantly, a majority of them report that they enjoy using the language through such activities!

Chapter 8 records Ho's experimental use of children's literature with her SM3 students. In addition to helping the PRC students understand and appreciate the content of some carefully chosen children's stories, Ho also uses such stories to teach the students literary styles and literary criticism. Students are encouraged to turn these stories into dramas and act out their re-creation in front of their classes. Sometimes reading-aloud exercises are done in class to help the students with their pronunciation difficulties. Ho finds that children's literature makes good readings for these young adults as the ease of content and language use may make English reading manageable, enjoyable, and achievable to these (temporarily) linguistically inadequate students. In fact, Ho suggests that other forms of children's literature, such as poems, novels and science fiction as well as adolescent literature may also be used with these pre-university PRC students to raise and sustain their reading interest.

In the next chapter, Ho discusses some specific pronunciation difficulties facing PRC students from different parts of China. Obviously, the different phonological systems in the different dialects of Chinese give rise to different areas of pronunciation difficulties. By examining her PRC students' videotaped oral presentations, Ho identifies /r, l, θ, ŋ, ʃ, tʃ/ as the most difficult consonants for the students in general and /k/ – /g/, /f/ – /v/, /t/ – /d/, and /p/ – /b/ as the most difficult consonant pairs. This finding largely conforms to other CELC teachers' perceptions about the PRC students' pronunciation difficulties with consonants. Some vowels and certain syllable structures in English are also identified as problematic to these students owing to their L1 transfer. With such specific trouble areas pinpointed, Ho then offers some useful teaching tips and strategies for teachers of PRC students to try out in the classroom.

Chapter 10 reports on some classroom research by Tan who implements learning strategy training in her graduate English course to see whether it enhances learner autonomy. By examining learners' diaries, Tan is able to trace the impact of the strategy training on the learning process of the PRC learners and the development of their metacognitive, cognitive, and social/affective strategies over time. Tan finds that with the introduction of the learning strategies, learners become more sophisticated and active in the learning process. They are also able to reflect on the learning methods they use and take more control over their learning goals. Tan concludes that strategy training "is suitable and needful for language learners from the PRC" (Tan, this volume: 187).

In the last chapter, Zhang and Li investigate the kind of learning strategies PRC students tend to use and the relationship between learners' use of such strategies and their English proficiency. Using the Strategy Inventory for Language Learning (SILL) developed by Oxford (1990), the authors find that like Chinese learners of English from Hong Kong, the SM3 students from China also use compensation and metacognitive strategies more than affective and memory strategies. The frequency of strategy use is also positively correlated with the learners' proficiency levels in general: The more the students use the learning strategies, the more progress they make in their various language skills. This finding echoes, to a certain extent, what Tan finds about the use of learning strategies by her postgraduate students from China (see Chapter 10). Zhang and Li, therefore, recommend learning strategy training in language classrooms to promote learner autonomy and enhance the learning process.

As there are more and more EFL/ESL Chinese learners of English in China and throughout the world, it becomes all the more important for language teachers to understand better the background of the students, their learning habits and their expectations. Although the studies in this book only report on the teaching experiences, classroom activities and the attitudes of the PRC students in Singapore, the book will, I believe, help language educators throughout the world to get to know PRC students better. The hands-on experience discussed in this book will provide a solid basis for language teachers and materials designers to write and implement more learner-specific teaching materials and appropriate teaching methods for PRC students in general.

Finally, a caveat is in order before I end this introduction. The language learning behaviours and patterns of Chinese learners of English reported in this book should not be overgeneralised or stereotyped as they are based on small groups of students in the classroom setting in one L2 environment. In fact, we have seen that various stereotypes about Chinese learners of English are called into question in some of the studies here. In Chapter 5, for example, Meyer found that contrary to general beliefs about Asian students' attitude towards group work, her PRC students have no objection to group work and do not prioritise group harmony over confrontation. So overgeneralisation should be strictly guarded against.

I recommend this book to everyone in the language teaching profession and in the field of second language acquisition research. In fact, anyone who is interested in language learning and teaching in general should have this book on his or her shelves.

Dr Yuan Yi
Division Head for Research
Centre for English Language Communication
National University of Singapore, 2002

REFERENCES

Crystal, David (1997). *English as a Global Language*. Cambridge: Cambridge University Press.

Golembeski, Daniel & Yuan, Yi (1995). Responding to compliments: A cross-linguistic study of the English pragmatics of Chinese, French, and English speakers. Paper presented at the 9th International Conference on Pragmatics and Language Learning. Urbana, Illinois.

Kachru, Braj B. (1982). *The Other Tongue: English Across Cultures*. Urbana: University of Illinois Press.

Kasper, Gabriele (1992). Pragmatic transfer. *Second Language Research*, 8(3): 203–231.

Kirkpatrick, Andy (1991). Information sequency in Mandarin letters of request. *Anthropological Linguistics*, 33(2): 183–203.

Larsen-Freeman, Diane (1986). *Techniques and Principles in Language Teaching*. Hong Kong: Oxford University Press.

Larsen-Freeman, Diane & Long, Michael H. (1991). *An Introduction to Second Language Acquisition Research*. London: Longman.

Oxford, R. (1990). *Language Learning Strategies: What Every Teacher Should Know*. Boston: Heinle & Heinle Publishers.

CHAPTER 1

In Search of Effective ELT Methodology in College English Education — The Chinese Experience

FENG ANWEI

INTRODUCTION

China undoubtedly has the largest undergraduate student population learning English as a foreign language. This population ranges from "real beginners" in the remote regions (Wu, 2000) to advanced learners who desire higher language proficiency than that required by the syllabus (He and Chen, 1996). The growing demand for English as a means to access modern technology and economic development in the past two decades has led to substantial changes in the teaching of English as a foreign language in China. ELT teaching models, conventional or contemporary, have been undergoing constant scrutiny and evaluation. Thus, the literature on ELT methodology is one of the largest with both theoretical discussions and reports of empirical research. Despite vigorous discussions in recent years, there seems to be no theoretical framework that is commonly believed to effectively suit the Chinese context of English language teaching. The large population of English learners of various levels and the ever-growing literature on this subject apparently make it difficult to discuss ELT methodology in China within the confines of this paper. Nevertheless, a general examination of ELT methodology is possible owing to the fact that in the last two decades the College English programme — the most important ELT programme for all college students, except English majors, in tertiary institutions — has been following the same syllabus and college students in most tertiary institutions have been using the same textbook. The review that follows will focus on the literature and official documents published or issued in this period. In order to gain a better understanding of College English education, let us first take a look at a teaching model that used to dominate, and still greatly influences, foreign language teaching in China.

THE INTENSIVE READING MODEL

Scholars in foreign language education (Fu, 1986; Li, Zhong and Liu, 1988) usually draw dividing lines in their discussions about the history of foreign language education in the five "post-liberation" decades (from 1949 till now) according to momentous political events. They seem to agree that major changes in foreign language education since 1949 have been due to the dynamics of politics in China. From 1949 to 1956, for instance, Russian was taught as the major foreign language because of China's close economic and diplomatic relationships with the former Soviet Union. With the door tightly closed to the Western world, many Western languages, particularly English which had been taught for a century, were almost stamped out (Li, Zhong and Liu, 1988). Starting from 1956 — when the country began its endeavour in constructing its own socialist version owing mainly to deteriorating relations with the Soviet Union — through to the onset of the Great Cultural Revolution, Russian gradually lost its popularity and English began to resume its status as a premium foreign language in the curriculum of tertiary education. In both periods, however, the so-called "intensive reading" course, developed under the influence of Russian methodologists (see Dzau, 1990: Chapter 3), was predominantly adopted for classroom teaching, although other teaching methods such as the direct model and the audio-lingual model developed overseas were experimented within specialised institutions for language majors (Li, 1995). The "intensive reading" course is now widely taken as the Chinese version of the grammar-translation model.

The term "intensive reading" needs defining as it is culture-specific. "Intensive reading" in the Chinese context refers to a highly teacher-centred course in which the teacher takes students through a text on a word-by-word and then sentence-by-sentence basis, explaining "language points" (new words and grammatical rules for classroom teaching and practising), leading pattern drills and translating difficult sentences in the text before engaging students with comprehension questions at the discourse level. Cortazzi and Jin (1996) explain that this teaching model became part of a Chinese culture of learning as for centuries the learning of Chinese followed the fixed order of dealing first with characters (*Zi*), words or phrases (*Ci*), sentences (*Jiu*) and paragraphs (*Duan*) before tackling the text (*Wen*). An intensive reading class usually begins with the teacher asking some students to read aloud certain paragraphs of a text and correcting pronunciation whenever necessary. This is followed by the main lesson when the teacher explains meticulously the vocabulary and grammatical points considered new to the students. The new words are usually associated with many other words such as synonyms and antonyms (*Cihui Kaihua*) and grammatical structures analysed and systemised (*Xitong Yufa*) (Wang, 1996). During the explanation, students are from time to time asked to answer short questions to test their comprehension, to use the new words and the grammatical points in language drills or to translate sentences. Usually, there is hardly any time in class for students to tackle comprehension questions on the text, let alone time for communicative activities. Thus, Cortazzi and Jin (1996) point out that the course is not primarily designed to improve reading comprehension as the name suggests. Rather, it is a course in which, using the text as a base, students learn vocabulary and grammar mainly through teacher exposition. Because of the meticulous explanation of language points by the teacher Wang (1996) recalls that it was often the case, particularly before the 1980s, that in an intensive reading course for English majors which usually took 6–8 hours per week, only about six texts were covered in a whole semester.

THE IMPACT OF THE "OPEN-DOOR" POLICY

The Great Cultural Revolution, the third period in foreign language education according to Fu (1986) and Li, Zhong and Liu (1988), started in 1966 and ended in 1976. During the first four years of the revolution from 1966 to 1970, China's higher education system virtually ceased functioning as tertiary institutions throughout the country stopped enrolling students. From 1971 to 1976 when most tertiary institutions resumed operation, English language was the dominating foreign language taught in universities while Russian was largely ignored. The political impact of the Cultural Revolution on foreign language education was so strong that EFL teaching was not foreign language teaching in its proper sense as it barely offered students anything other than the English version of political slogans or quotations of Mao Zedong, the then paramount leader of China (Fu, 1986). Ideological orientation was the primary concern of policy makers, textbook writers, methodologists and teachers of all foreign language courses during this period.

The fourth period began in 1977, the year after the Cultural Revolution when the education of the country was back to normal. From that year onwards, China became increasingly exposed to the outside world, particularly the Western countries. Owing to its "open-door" policies, its awareness of the importance of English as a means of international commerce and communications increased accordingly. From 1977 to 1984, ELT methods and teaching materials were gradually liberalised as many native speaker teachers were invited into the country and many textbooks written by Western EFL/ESL writers were imported and used in classrooms. Most importantly, in this period, according to Li, Zhong and Liu (1988), theoretical concepts in psycholinguistics, sociolinguistics and applied linguistics developed in Western countries created a strong impact on conventional ideas of foreign language teaching in China. The intensive reading model was under severe criticism, particularly from English native speakers teaching in China such as Cotton (1990) and Maley (1990), and the communicative language teaching approach (see the next two sections below for details) drew much attention from ELT methodologists and teachers.

THE 1985 SYLLABUS AND *BO CAI ZHONG CHANG*

ELT specialists agree that China has experienced the greatest development in foreign language education since the *College English Syllabus* (College English Syllabus Revision Team, 1985) was promulgated by the then State Education Commission in 1985. Han, Lu and Dong (1995), for instance, claim that the promulgation of the syllabus has resulted in many major breakthroughs in higher education in general and English language education in particular. They quote Zhou Yuanqin, Director of the Higher Education Division of the Ministry of Education, as saying,

> College English is the most substantial programme in the country. It attracts the greatest attention of our students. The programme is decisive in the country's education reform and the two (College English) tests are influential in the country.
>
> (Han, Lu and Dong, 1995: 45, my translation)

The syllabus, according to Han (1985, 1999), a College English specialist cum policy maker, incorporates the merits of many communicative language teaching models developed by Western scholars. Theoretically, the syllabus integrates the principles in Brumfit's (1984) discussions on communicative language teaching methodology in balancing language usage and use and in mediating accuracy and fluency in foreign language education. For practical ideas, the syllabus acknowledges van Ek (1976) as the main reference for the "functional and notional inventory". Han (1999) observes that the "inventory of micro-skills" of language use is nearly a direct copy of the "taxonomy of language skills" listed in Munby (1978: 123–31). The "ultimate goal" of the College English programme, the syllabus specifies, is to develop students' competence to communicate in the target language via written and oral channels. In the syllabus, while linguistic competence is referred to as "the ability to use one's knowledge of the language to comprehend and construct sentences", communicative competence is defined as "the ability to employ appropriate skills at discourse level to acquire and convey information" (College English Syllabus Revision Team, 1985: 267). The syllabus states that the emphasis in the teaching process should gradually move from skills training at the sentence level towards communicative training at the discourse level.

As specific course objectives, the syllabus stipulates that the "chief aim" of the College English course is to develop in students strong reading skills so as to enable them to acquire information in their own fields of specialisation. Skills in listening and translation are ranked as the second level requirement while writing and speaking skills are ranked as the least required for the course takers. In the syllabus, a needs analysis survey conducted in 1983 is mentioned briefly to justify the ranking of the five language skills.

As for teaching methodology, the syllabus propounds the notion "*Bo Cai Zhong Chang*" (assimilating merits of different teaching approaches for our own use), suggesting clearly in this context a vision outward, that is, to move from the traditional intensive reading model developed at home to the communicative language teaching approach which originated from Western countries. Since the promulgation of the syllabus, the literature on methodology has shown a distinctive focus on communicative language teaching theories and practices.

AN OVERVIEW OF CLASSROOM METHODOLOGY

Han, Lu and Dong (1995), three of the most senior figures (policy makers cum College English textbook writers) in College English education, specify three features of the communicative language teaching approach for the Chinese context. First, it develops the teacher-centred activity model (the "intensive reading" model, my interpretation) into a student-centred one. Second, it moves from the TALO (text as linguistic object) approach to the TAVI (text as vehicle for information) approach, a clear reference to the TALO/TAVI distinction made by Johns and Davies (1983). And third, it uses the target language as the medium of instruction in classrooms. Many other College English educators (for example, Guo, 1995) assert that the major feature of the communicative language teaching approach is its strong emphasis on oral skills. In a typical communicative classroom the main task of teaching is to organise oral activities such as role play and group discussions. Since the promulgation of the 1985 syllabus, some College English teachers have discussed the effectiveness of different communicative methods they have experimented with in their classrooms. Zhang (1995), for example, believes that the major task for a College English teacher is to transform the classroom, where transmission of knowledge is both the process and the aim, into one that enables learners to start communicating. In his "intensive reading" classes, on the premise that essential grammatical input had been given to students, he involved his students in many communicative tasks such as group discussion, presentation, story retelling, role-play, etc. to help them improve both linguistic and communicative skills. The teaching, he reports, became both meaningful and motivating and the syllabus requirements for the language skills were better fulfilled. All three features listed in Han, Lu and Dong (1995) and the major feature specified in Guo (1995) are apparently present in Zhang's practice. In a similar manner, Ma (1998) demonstrates how he used the communicative approach to grammar teaching to students taking College English courses.

"Success stories" like this, however, seem rare in publications and in many studies of College English classrooms. To find out if a shift from the traditional intensive reading model to communicative language teaching has really taken place, Zheng, Wei and Chen (1997) carried out a large-scale questionnaire survey among 351 teachers and 3,224 students from 20 tertiary institutions. In this survey, the teachers were asked to estimate how long they spent in each class "instructing" students. Similarly, the students were asked to estimate how long their teachers spent in each class "talking to them". Tables 1 and 2 present the statistics from this survey. They found that most of the classrooms were very teacher-centred.

About two-thirds of the teachers estimated that they used more than 60% of classroom time explaining vocabulary and sentences and teaching grammar. The percentage given by the students about teachers' talking time was even higher than the self-estimation of the teachers. Nearly 75% of the students estimated that their teachers' talking time

Table 1. Teachers' Replies to "How Much Time Do You Spend Instructing in Class?" (n = 351)

% of time talking	Number of answers	% of answers
No answer	25	7.1
21–40	13	3.7
41–60	74	21.1
61–80	160	45.6
80 & above	79	22.5

Table 2. Students' Replies to "How Much Time Does Your Teacher Spend Talking to You in Class?" (n = 3,224)

% of time talking	Number of answers	% of answers
21–40	177	5.5
41–60	645	20.0
61–80	1254	38.9
80 & above	1148	35.6

Source: Zheng, Wei and Chen (1997: 2–3).

was 60% or more, and more than a third of them even thought more than 80% of the class time was "teacher talk".

To further confirm the statistical findings the researchers conducted classroom observations and interviews. They noted that in College English classrooms the majority of teachers kept on explaining language points, grammar in difficult sentences and translating long sentences while their students mainly remained passive, listening and taking notes. Some often made their students practise on mock test papers, checked spelling of students' writing and gave dictation. The tools for classroom teaching remained traditional: a textbook, a piece of chalk and a blackboard though the use of language laboratories was found to be rising. Few classes, they noted, were conducted in the communicative language teaching approach as commonly defined.

In another recent survey, similar observations were made. With the purpose of analysing the quality and quantity of "teacher talk", Zhao (1998) managed to observe and record a number of reading classroom interactions between teachers and students. After analysing the recorded data she reported findings, both quantitative and qualitative, of eight cases that she claimed to be representative. She provided evidence that College English classrooms were teacher-centred and transmission of knowledge still featured prominently in classroom practice. She noted that some teachers made clear attempts to interact with their students during their "teacher talk". However, the interactions were predominantly closed questions raised by the teacher eliciting simple answers from the students. Open-ended questions by the teacher and interactions between students were almost non-existent.

In recent discussions of methodological trends in College English education, there does not seem to be any report showing empirical evidence that the course moves, as claimed in Han, Lu and Dong (1995), from the TALO (text as linguistic object) approach to the TAVI (text as vehicle for information) approach. Oral activities such as role play and group discussion stated as the major feature of the communicative approach (Guo, 1995) are also rare in College English classrooms according to observations by researchers such as Zhao (1998) and Zheng, Wei and Chen (1997).

Nevertheless, both Zhao (1998) and Zheng, Wei and Chen (1997) reported that the third feature of communicative language teaching, as identified by Han, Lu and Dong (1995) existed in many College English classrooms. An increasing number of teachers began using the

Table 3.   Teacher's Responses to the Question on the Medium of Instruction
(n = 351)

Medium of instruction	No. of people	% of people
No answer	26	7.4
Always in Chinese	2	0.6
Almost always in Chinese	3	0.9
Mostly in Chinese	27	7.7
Half in Chinese and half in English	74	21.1
Mostly in English	125	35.6
Almost always in English	85	24.6
Always in English	9	2.6

target language as the medium of instruction. Table 3 shows how the teachers responded to the question, "Which language do you use as the medium of instruction?" in Zheng, Wei and Chen's (1997) survey. These figures, they pointed out, show that the medium of instruction is in contrast with that of two decades ago when almost all lessons were conducted in Chinese. The slow but evident change in the medium of instruction is often seen as a breakaway from the traditional grammar-translation model.

CONTEXTUAL FACTORS

Empirical research findings and observations in recent literature strongly suggest that except for a gradual change in the medium of instruction, major features of the traditional grammar-translation or intensive-reading model are still predominant in the majority of College English classrooms. Classroom teaching is teacher-centred and transmission of knowledge remains the standard practice as well as an educational aim. The communicative language teaching approach as defined by Han, Lu and Dong (1995) is not adopted. In many recent papers College English specialists have explicitly or implicitly questioned the value of the approach. These writers have attributed the poor accuracy shown in students' essays and oral skills to the communicative approach. They argue that years of teaching practice since the promulgation of the syllabus has shown that the communicative approach does not work in the Chinese context for these reasons:

1. *The communicative approach does not address "Chinese characteristics"[1].*

In Guo's (1995) list of "Chinese characteristics" of foreign language education, he firmly states that Chinese students are used to teacher-centred lessons whereby they expect teachers to explain words, sentences and texts in detail in class. Guo further states that students often feel disconcerted when they have to perform tasks such as classroom discussions and role-play. Cortazzi and Jin's (1996) study is in general agreement with Guo's statement though they use the notion "the culture of learning", defined as culturally-based ideas about appropriate learning styles, valued classroom behaviour and also about effective teaching, as against Guo's "Chinese characteristics" which implies a socio-political orientation.

2. *In College English education, priority should be given to linguistic or grammatical competence so as to build up a foundation for students to eventually use the language to acquire information.*

Han, Lu and Dong (1995) observe that, because of an over-emphasis on communicative methodology in recent years, College English teachers tend to neglect the necessity to develop grammatical competence in students. The numerous errors in essays give evidence that the students are weaker than their predecessors in spelling, grammar and vocabulary. They argue strongly that to achieve the "ultimate goal" (refer to the section on the 1985 syllabus above) the development of students' linguistic ability should take the priority in College English education. Basic training in pronunciation and spelling and basic grammatical knowledge should be regarded as the primary task in College English teaching. Without a solid foundation of these linguistic abilities, the development of communicative competence can only be an illusion.

---

[1] The notion of "Chinese characteristics" has been widely used as a political catchphrase since the former paramount leader of China, Deng Xiaoping, had his book "Build socialism with Chinese characteristics" published (Deng, 1985). The use of the notion usually carries the socio-political connotation though the arguments presented in Guo (1995) are mainly socio-cultural.

3. The teaching approach is largely determined by what is tested.

The "backwash" effects of the two nation-wide College English tests on College English education have been most vigorously discussed in recent papers (Wang, 1991; Zha, 1995; and Feng, 1995). These two tests are coded CET 4 (College English Test for Band 4) and CET 6 (College English Test for Band 6) respectively and they are administered semi-annually. CET 4 is taken by almost all students because the first four band courses are stipulated in the syllabus as the courses leading to the "basic required achievement level" for the programme (College English Syllabus Revision Team, 1985: 2–3). CET 6 is taken only by those who, after CET 4, continue to do the "upper required achievement level" courses (College English Syllabus Revision Team, 1985: 4). The passing rates of students taking the tests have become increasingly important to every tertiary institution because as the statistics are published in official documents, the comparative statistical data have a clear implication for the academic reputation of individual tertiary institutions. As a result, enabling students to pass the tests has been the primary concern of teachers and authorities of many tertiary institutions. In these institutions, a pass in CET 4 is a prerequisite for graduation and the pass rates of students are linked with the promotion prospects of individual teachers. Teaching is, therefore, test-oriented. It is a common observation that, in the semester when students prepare for CET 4, they are made to spend most of their class time practising numerous mock exam papers. Oral communication skills are generally ignored as they are not tested.

4. Teachers use the textbook as their syllabus to guide their lesson planning.

The need to cover the substantial textbook materials often makes it difficult to carry out communicative activities in the classroom (Zhao, 1998). The *Intensive Reading* booklets of the most widely-used textbook series, *College English* (a series of 54 booklets edited by Dong *et al.*, 1997), are a slightly modified version of the same title first published in 1986. They are largely grammar-structure and vocabulary-based course books which most teachers use with traditional methodology. The *Teacher's Book* for each of the four "core" *Intensive Reading* booklets contains, in each text, a large number of "language points" — basically grammar and vocabulary items for detailed explanation in class. Even though some communicative activities are suggested, the presentation of language points regarded as essential content for explanation usually takes a lot of classroom time and invariably makes the teacher take centre stage in the classroom leaving the students to listen passively (Zhao, 1998; Zheng, Wei and Chen, 1997).[2]

5. College English teachers are not ready to adopt the approach for classroom practice.

Despite clear indications in the syllabus to use the communicative approach and vigorous discussions by its advocators, teachers seem to believe that the communicative methodology is not realistic for the Chinese classroom. Xia (1999) reports that in recent years she has made attempts to promote communicative methods to teacher trainees and students. She notes that most of the trainees and students have shown a positive attitude towards the communicative approach. Ironically, nearly all of these trainees and students question the feasibility of this approach for Chinese classroom practice.

There are many other contextual factors identified by College English educators as causes for the failure of the communicative methodology in the Chinese context. The huge linguistic and socio-cultural differences between the target language and learners' own; inadequate training teachers received in using communicative methods in classroom situations; the large number of students in each classroom and even the physical design of seating (in most classrooms seats are fixed to the floor in rows) are all presented as factors which hinder the smooth running of communicative activities.

---

[2] Of the 54 booklets, the first four *Intensive Reading* booklets are taken as the 'core' materials for College English teaching mainly because they incorporate all the required elements contained in the four inventories (vocabulary, grammar, micro-skills and functions/notions) in the syllabus, in which reading skills are stipulated as the most required. *The Teacher's Book* for the four *Intensive Reading* booklets, therefore, show the editors' teaching philosophy with suggested guidelines for teaching. All the other booklets, such as *Extensive Reading*, are of secondary importance and are mostly assigned as homework. In class, the teacher may give answers to the questions in those booklets.

It should be noted that some discussions on the learning and socio-political contexts of College English education are rather speculative and intuitive. Many scholars such as Guo (1995), for example, show a strong belief that Chinese students disliked oral activities such as classroom discussions and role-play because they were used to passive learning. Empirical evidence given by researchers such as Feng (1998) and Zheng, Wei and Chen (1997), however, shows that students were generally aware of the importance of oral skills and keen on participating actively in oral activities. Similarly, there are different speculative views held by researchers on teacher training in the communicative methods. But the main thrust of the arguments in the many observations made by teacher trainers such as Xia (1999) and Crook (1990) indicates that it is the educational philosophy held by the trainees and their attitude towards the communicative approach, rather than the training they have received, that keep them from adopting communicative methods in classrooms.

LOOKING FOR ALTERNATIVES

Doubts on the communicative language teaching approach in recent years has, not surprisingly, led ELT methodologists to look for alternative ways of teaching. The flexible implication of the slogan, *"Bo Cai Zhong Chang"* has allowed some College English specialists such as Li (1995) and Gu (1997) to further claim that "there is no set methodology for teaching" (*Jiao Wu Ding Fa*). They argue that given the context of College English education the teaching programme should not follow any particular methodology, no matter how theoretically established it is, and teachers as individuals need to be flexible, innovative and creative. Other specialists, however, continue their efforts in seeking theoretically sound methodologies for College English. Qin (1996) reviewed the feasibility of the "whole language approach" for use in the Chinese situation. Three years later, Qin (1999) recommended the "double activities approach" developed by Wang (1996) on the basis of the "integrated approach" adopted for secondary schools in Singapore, the "activities-based approach" designed in Australia and the theoretical "balanced activities approach" proposed by Harmer (1983). Xia and Kong (1998) compared the "difficulty-based teaching method" and the "task-based teaching method" developed in Western countries with the traditional teaching approach dominant in China and suggested that the two methods could help learners explore their own potentials and address the new demands for education in the new century. A "thematic-teaching model" designed and tested on a small scale is detailed in Ying, He and Zhou (1998). The literature of these methodology "proposals" shows that the majority of them are again modelled from communicative language teaching principles.

THE 1999 SYLLABUS

In 1994 after nearly a decade of implementation of the 1985 College English syllabus, policy makers and College English specialists decided that the syllabus needed to be revised "in order to face the challenge of the new century and to raise College English teaching to a new level" (College English Revision Team, 1999: 175, my translation). The new syllabus was finally promulgated at the end of 1999 after five years of revision. Han (1999) pinpoints in the new syllabus, several changes made to the 1985 version. The most obvious change is that the "ultimate goal" stipulated in the 1985 version to develop students' communicative competence is entirely missing from the new version. The general objective of the programme has evolved into "to develop in students strong reading skills and certain levels of listening, speaking, writing and translating competence so as to enable them to *exchange information* in English" (College English Revision Team, 1999: 1, my translation and italics). Even the term, *communicative competence*, is replaced by a new notion, *Yingyong Nengli*, which could be translated into "competence for application". The changes in the general teaching aim and terminology clearly suggest a redirection in teaching philosophy.

What remains unchanged is the ranking of reading skills. As in the 1985 syllabus, reading skills are stipulated as the most essential of all language skills in the revised syllabus. Such ranking has long been challenged by College English researchers and teachers with empirical findings (Ying, 1996; Xia, 1997; Huang and Shao, 1998). These researchers have conducted large-scale surveys among graduates and employers. On the basis of the empirical evidence that oral skills are regarded by these two groups of people as the most important of all language skills, they strongly argue that the syllabus should at least attach equal importance to the development of all language skills. In a recent paper, Zeng and Zhang (1999) reveal that, according to a "Revision Explanation" which they were "lucky to have access to", this ranking was based on a survey conducted among "officials" and teachers as these two groups regarded reading skills as the most important. They argue that the validity, reliability and practicability of the survey are problematic because it ignored the views of graduates and employers, the most pertinent informants as far as the future needs of the students are concerned. The "Revision Explanation" critiqued by Zeng and Zhang (1999) suggests that, in needs analysis, perceptions of "officials" (policy makers) about the future needs of learners are final as policy makers would certainly view the needs in connection with the general educational aims and with the political and socio-economical needs of the country. This is a crucial socio-political dimension that foreign language educators have to take into consideration for curriculum planning. The teachers' ranking of reading skills as the most important, as given in the "Revision Explanation", is equally revealing as it indicates that reading is highly valued by Chinese language educators. The "Revision Explanation" re-establishes the point that foreign language education always takes place in a particular context and the aims of language programmes are always politically determined (Byram, 1997). A thorough analysis of the learning and socio-political contexts is thus a prerequisite for meaningful curriculum planning for ELT programmes.

As for teaching methodology, the new syllabus gives no indication of which methodology is to be adopted but makes a call for searching out a methodology with "Chinese characteristics":

> The teaching methods developed at home and abroad are all products created in specific circumstances and for specific contexts. We must, of course, learn from valuable experience and advanced teaching methodology developed abroad. More importantly, however, we must sum up the effective teaching methods and experience accumulated at home and appropriately mediate the relationship between making use (of foreign experiences) and carrying forward (our traditions). We must base ourselves upon our own situation and reality and seek a new ELT approach with Chinese characteristics.
>
> (College English Revision Team, 1999: 11, my translation)

The need of *"Bo Cai Zhong Chang"* (assimilating merits of different teaching methodologies for our own use) does not seem to be fundamentally changed. The tone, however, suggests a strong desire for developing a teaching methodology of Chinese identity and thus a need to re-evaluate traditional models developed at home and reassess the outward vision shown in the 1985 syllabus, that is, to favour the communicative language teaching approach.

CONCLUSION

Methodological discussions in recent years and the evidence shown in official documents clearly suggest that the methodology is dependent upon many interrelated factors which include the socio-political context, the culture of learning, the testing system and the educational philosophy of textbook producers. In most College English classrooms in China, the intensive reading model, though slightly altered under the impact of the communicative approach in recent years, has remained the main teaching mode simply because it has addressed these contextual issues more effectively than the communicative approach. First of all, the model is taken as one developed at home and thus suits the deeply rooted culture of learning in which transmission of knowledge is seen as the main task of classroom teaching (Cortazzi and Jin, 1996). Second, the model puts clear emphasis on the "three basic language elements" — pronunciation, vocabulary and grammar — which are considered the prerequisites for strong reading competence, the most important among all language skills as perceived by College English policy makers and teachers and the first-ranked objective for the course. Third, the majority of College English teachers were trained in the intensive reading model and they are, in Guo's (1995) words, "used to teaching texts as linguistic objects". These teachers, in general, believe that learning a foreign language is a linear and accumulative process and its success depends upon a solid foundation of vocabulary and grammar. Finally, to do well in crucial tests such as CET 4, students believe they need only develop reading skills and grammatical competence.

Despite these contextual factors in favour of traditional models, recent critical reviews of the communicative approach and the call made in the new syllabus to reassess traditional methodology, the slogan, *Bo Cai Zhong Chang*, stays firm as few teachers and language education scholars seem to strongly believe that the intensive reading model is the methodological framework for China. Some Chinese ELT educators such as Fan (1999) argue that the most appropriate model is likely to be an "eclectic" model which is defined as "ideal", having developed from a selection of well-grounded models including the existing model and taking into consideration contextual factors such as time, location and types of learners. In the syllabus of the programme for English majors, the title of the main course has been changed from the traditional "intensive reading" to "integrated English". Wang (1996) points out that the change of the course title should not be taken simply as a wording issue. This change symbolises a reformation of teaching philosophy and suggests an integration of teaching approaches. I share Wang's view that there should be an integration of teaching approaches. I also agree with Fan (1999) that the realistic model comes from realisation and modification of current practice. Both Fan and Wang clearly advocate a true *Bo Cai Zhong Chang* attitude. It seems clear that the course title change made in the syllabus for English majors is also necessary for College English as it is obviously the first step in the direction of an integration of teaching approaches. As indicated in the section on contextual factors, I further argue that systematic and comprehensive studies need to be carried out to gain further insight into the learning and socio-political contexts of the College English programme. It is with this insight that ELT educators in China are more likely to develop a theoretically grounded model for College English, one which truly assimilates the merits of different ELT teaching approaches (*Bo Cai Zhong Chang*).

With the ever-growing number of PRC students and professionals taking English courses in Singapore, an examination of ELT methodology in China has become all the more relevant to our teaching practice here. Knowledge of the teaching models widely used in China, for example, would help us better understand our PRC students' expectations of classroom activities. Similarly, familiarity with the *College English Syllabus* and the objectives stipulated in it could increase our awareness of the English background of our PRC postgraduate students and professionals working in Singapore as the majority, if not all, have completed the required courses of the College English programme. But, to what extent this knowledge or insight can be incorporated into our curriculum planning, classroom teaching, material development and assessment is obviously beyond the scope of this paper. For curriculum planning, for instance, all the "Chinese characteristics" discussed above ought to be thoroughly reviewed in connection with the Singapore context, the short-term and long-term needs of our PRC students and the Singaporean culture of learning. This paper, from this perspective, presents a new dimension for reflecting on our existing practice.

REFERENCES*

Brumfit, C. J. (1984). *Communicative Methodology in Language Teaching*. Cambridge: Cambridge University Press.

Byram, M. (1997). *Teaching and Assessing Intercultural Communicative Competence*. Clevedon, England: Multilingual Matters Ltd.

Chen, T. H. E. (1981). *Chinese Education since 1949: Academic and Revolutionary Models*. New York: Pergamon Press.

College English Syllabus Revision Team (1985). *College English Syllabus (CES): Applicable to Undergraduates of Science and Engineering*. Beijing: Higher Education Press.

_____ (1999). *College English Syllabus (CES): Applicable to Undergraduates of Tertiary Institutions*. Beijing: Higher Education Press and Shanghai: Shanghai Foreign Language Education Press.

Cortazzi, M. & Jin, L. (1996). Cultures of learning: Language classrooms in China. In H. Coleman (Ed.), *Society in the Language Classroom* (pp. 169–205). Cambridge: Cambridge University Press.

Cotton, I. (1990). Why intensive reading hinders the development of both English language teaching and English language learning in China. *Teaching English in China; ELT Newsletter*, 20: 49–52. Beijing: British Council.

Crook, D. (1990). Some problems of Chinese education as seen through the eyes of a foreigner. In Z. Wang *et al.* (Eds.), *ELT in China: Papers Presented at ISTEC, Guangzhou, China* (pp. 29–38). Beijing: Foreign Language Teaching and Research Press.

Deng, X. P. (1985). *Build Socialism with Chinese Characteristics*. Beijing: Foreign Languages Press.

Dong, Y. F. *et al.* (Eds.) (1997). *College English* (a series of 54 booklets). Shanghai: Shanghai Foreign Languages Education Press.

Dzau, Y. F. (Ed.) (1990). *English in China*. Hong Kong: API Press.

Fan, C. R. (1999). Eclecticism in second/foreign language teaching. *Waiyu Jiaoxue Yu Yanjiu* (Foreign Language Teaching and Research), 118(2): 29–34.

---

* When the title of a book or a journal is given in *Chinese pinyin*, the book or the article in the journal is always written in Chinese.

Feng, M. (1995). A survey of the psychological factors in learning English among students of science and engineering. *Waiyu Jiaoxue Yu Yanjiu* (Foreign Language Teaching and Research), 102(2): 54–57.

_____ (1998). An investigation into the English study of students in colleges and universities of science and engineering. *Wai Yu Jie* (Journal of the Foreign Language World), 69(1): 23–27.

Fu, K. (1986). *Zhongguo Waiyu Jiaoyu Shi* (The History of Foreign Language Education in China). Shanghai: Shanghai Foreign Language Education Press.

Guo, J. K. (1995). Improve classroom teaching and raise CET to a new plateau. *Wai Yu Jie* (Journal of the Foreign Language World), 57(1): 50–53.

Gu, S. Y. (1997). On approaches to ELT in China. *Wai Yu Jie* (Journal of the Foreign Language World), 65(1): 3–6.

Han, Q. S. (1985). Syllabus design and features of College English Syllabus. *Wai Yu Jie* (Journal of the Foreign Language World), 19(4): 4–6.

_____ (1999). On the teaching syllabus of College English. *Wai Yu Jie* (Journal of the Foreign Language World), 76(4): 21–23.

Han, Q. S.; Lu, C. & Dong, Y. F. (1995). Fully implement the syllabus and improve teaching quality. *Wai Yu Jie* (Journal of the Foreign Language World), 57(1): 44–49.

Harmer, J. (1983). *The Practice of English Language Teaching*. London: Longman.

He, C. Y. & Chen, M. S. (1996). Adjusting teaching goals to suit the objective needs. *Wai Yu Jie* (Journal of the Foreign Language World), 58(2): 23–28.

Huang, J. B. & Shao, Y. Z. (1998). Prospect of reforms in college English teaching. *Wai Yu Jie* (Journal of Foreign Language World), 72(4): 20–22.

Johns, T. & Davies, F. (1983). Text as a vehicle for information: The classroom use of written texts in teaching reading in a foreign language. *Reading in a Foreign Language*, 1(1): 1–19.

Li, L. Y.; Zhong, R. X. & Liu, L. (Eds.) (1988). *Zhongguo Yingyu Jiaoyushi* (A History of English Language Teaching in China). Shanghai: Shanghai Foreign Languages Education Press.

Li, Y. H. (1995). Improving the quality of classroom teaching is our current major concern. *Wai Yu Jie* (Journal of the Foreign Language World), 57(1): 54–57.

Ma, Z. (1998). On the communicative approach to teaching College English grammar. *Wai Yu Jie* (Journal of the Foreign Language World), 69(1): 44–46.

Maley, A. (1990). XANADU — A miracle of rare device: The teaching of English in China. In Y. F. Dzau (Ed.), *English in China* (pp. 95–105). Hong Kong: API Press.

Munby, J. (1978). Communicative Syllabus Design: A Sociolinguistic Model for Defining the Content of Purpose-specific Language Programmes. Cambridge: Cambridge University Press.

Qin, X. G. (1996). A review of the 'whole language approach'. *Wai Yu Jie* (Journal of the Foreign Language World), 62(2): 13–17.

_____ (1999). Building up a new English teaching model with Chinese features. *Wai Yu Jie* (Journal of the Foreign Language World), 75(3): 19–23.

van Ek, J. (1976). *The Threshold Level for Modern Language Teaching in Schools*. Groningen, Netherlands: Longman.

Wang, C. R. (1996). *Yingyu Jiaoxue Jiaojilun* (A communication model for English Language teaching). Nannin: Guangxi Educational Press.

Wang, J. J. (1991). Rectifying the relationship between the syllabus, teaching and testing and strengthening the administration of College English teaching. *Wai Yu Jie* (Journal of the Foreign Language World), 43(special issue): 21–24.

Wu, X. Q. (2000). On College English teaching from the preliminary stage for students of minority nationalities in Xin Jiang. *Wai Yu Jie* (Journal of the Foreign Language World), 77(1): 41–43.

Xia, J. M. (1997). Reflections on the development of College English textbooks for the new century. In Y. Hou & Z. Lu (Eds.), *Qinhua Waiyu Jiaoyu Luncong* (Working papers of foreign language education in Qinhua) (pp. 51–68). Beijing: Qinhua University.

————— (1999). Adhere to the practical approach to College English teaching. *Wai Yu Jie* (Journal of the Foreign Language World), 76(4): 31–37.

Xia, J. M. & Kong, X. H. (1998). Theoretical basis of 'difficulty-based teaching method' and 'task-based teaching method' and comparison of the two modes. *Wai Yu Jie* (Journal of the Foreign Language World), 72(4): 34–40.

Ying, H. L. (1996). Theoretical grounds and social bases of syllabus design. *Wai Yu Jie* (Journal of the Foreign Language World), 62(2): 41–45.

Ying, H.; He, L. & Zhou, S. (1998). Reflections on the teaching of English to non-English majors. *Waiyu Jiaoxue Yu Yanjiu* (Foreign Language Teaching and Research), 116(4): 22–26.

Zeng, X. G. & Zhang, J. H. (1999). A defect in the revision explanation of the syllabus. *Waiyu yu Waiyu Jiaoxue* (Foreign Languages and Foreign Language Teaching), 116(1): 52–53.

Zha, L. S. (1995). Fully implement the teaching syllabus and improve the quality of college English teaching. *Wai Yu Jie* (Journal of the Foreign Language World), 59(3): 24–27.

Zhang, Y. C. (1995). Improving students' communicative competence in the intensive English course. *Wai Yu Jie* (Journal of the Foreign Language World), 59(3): 28–31.

Zhao, X. H. (1998). A study of teacher talk in CE reading classes. *Wai Yu Jie* (Journal of the Foreign Language World), 70(2): 17–22.

Zheng, S.; Wei, N. & Chen, R. (1997). Research work on CE teaching methodology. *Wai Yu Jie* (Journal of the Foreign Language World), 67(3): 1–7.

CHAPTER 2

Learner Diaries as a Tool to Heighten Chinese Students' Metacognitive Awareness of English Learning

CARISSA YOUNG & FONG YOKE SIM

INTRODUCTION

Learner autonomy literature has suggested that language learners have their own beliefs, opinions and concepts about language learning. They have a repertoire of strategies for various language tasks (Wenden, 1986; Nunan, 1988). This "know-how" of language learning is called *metacognitive knowledge*, which is referred to as "the stable, statable although sometimes incorrect knowledge that learners have acquired about language, learning and the language learning process; also referred to as knowledge or concepts about language learning or learner beliefs" (Wenden, 1991: 163). There are three main types of metacognitive knowledge: *person knowledge, strategic knowledge* and *task knowledge.* Person knowledge includes what learners know about how they process information and what they know about themselves as language learners. Strategic knowledge is the general knowledge learners have about the nature of a strategy, and how a strategy can be used effectively (Wenden, 1991). Task knowledge refers to what learners know about the nature of language and communication, and what they need to know about a specific task such as its purpose, demands and degree of difficulties (Wenden, 1995). An awareness of one's metacognitive knowledge is referred to as *metacognitive awareness.* By raising their metacognitive awareness, learners become more active and independent in their learning process (Wenden, 1991; Chamot and O'Malley, 1994).

One way to heighten language learners' metacognitive awareness is to have them reflect upon their language learning processes regularly by keeping a learner diary, which is defined as "a first-person account of a language learning or teaching experience, documented through regular, candid entries in a personal journal" (Bailey, 1990: 215). Diary-keeping has been included in some learner training curricula as a self-assessment exercise (Nunan, 1988; Ellis and Sinclair, 1989; Chamot and O'Malley, 1994).

Previous work with learner diaries has shown that diary-keeping helps learners become more aware of their language learning. A study conducted in Japan examined 36 diary entries kept by one Japanese student while she was enrolled in an eight-week intensive English course (Matsumoto, 1989). Analysis of the diaries showed that the student became more aware of factors like praise from teachers, competition among classmates and anxiety which affected her language learning. The awareness of these "personal factors" (similar to person knowledge in this study), however, could not be generalised because of the small sample size and short period of data collection. Regarding language learners' knowledge of strategy use, Nunan (1996) asked 60 Chinese ESL students to keep a guided learner diary during a 12-week English course. It was found that these students gradually focused more on language content and learning processes. A comparison of a few extracts at the beginning and the end of the course showed that the students could describe their strategy use more accurately and at greater length over time. However, the students' person knowledge and task knowledge development were not examined. In Singapore, Goh (1997) analysed the weekly diaries kept by 40 Chinese EFL students over a period of 10 weeks and identified 63 sub-categories of metacognitive knowledge in listening. The study did not focus on how diaries helped the learners raise their metacognitive awareness in listening.

Although the above papers have claimed that learner diaries are helpful in raising learners' metacognitive awareness, few published papers have illustrated how diaries reflect the trends of learners' metacognitive knowledge development. This paper will, therefore, illustrate how learner diaries might help Chinese students heighten their metacognitive awareness of EFL learning over time. It is hoped that the results reported in this paper would help language teachers better understand the metacognitive knowledge development of EFL learners.

METHOD

Subjects

This diary study involved 38 students (31 males and 7 females) from the People's Republic of China. They were 19 years old on average and had been studying English for six years prior to enrolling in an intensive English course conducted by the National University of Singapore under the auspices of the Singapore Ministry of Education. They underwent this six-month intensive English course to prepare themselves for tertiary studies. These students had classes for five and a half hours a day from Monday through Friday between December 1997 and June 1998. They belonged to two tutorial groups, each of which was taught by one of the authors and four other tutors. This meant that the students normally met each of their tutors once a week.

Procedures

At the beginning of the course, each student was given a file which contained a diary (with detachable sheets of paper) and guidelines for diary writing. They were asked to record their English learning experiences by completing the following sentences every teaching week (adapted from Nunan, 1988: 134):

> This week I learned...
> This week I spoke English with...
> This week I made these mistakes...
> This week I knew these things about Singapore...
> My difficulties are...
> I would like to know...
> My English learning plans for next week are...

The students were given guidelines so that they could document their English learning experiences within a framework and avoid giving irrelevant information (Nunan, 1996; Goh, 1997).

The students gave the authors oral permission to analyse their diaries anonymously. They wrote their diary entries on the loose sheets and submitted one entry per week to the authors. These diary entries were read by the authors and returned to the students a week later. For research purposes, the diary entries were photocopied with permission. By the end of the course, 698 diary entries had been collected.

Data Analysis

The diary entries were coded for the identification of metacognitive knowledge using the classification scheme proposed by Wenden (1991). The original scheme consisted of three main categories and eight sub-categories of metacognitive knowledge. In this study, some modifications were made to classify and define the metacognitive knowledge revealed in the learner diaries. Two additional sub-categories of strategic knowledge were added. One of these new sub-categories, *possible strategies for improving skills*, represents the learners' knowledge about the strategies that they would probably use to improve their language skills. The second new sub-category, *evaluation of strategy use*, refers to the students' comments on a certain strategy that they had used. Appendix A shows the classification scheme developed for the present study.

The metacognitive knowledge classification scheme was used to code the diary data. Every remark that revealed a student's metacognitive knowledge of English learning was highlighted and the sub-category of metacognitive knowledge was written in the margin of the student's diary sheet. Using this scheme, the authors coded all the diary entries written by their own students.

To check the consistency of coding, both authors coded ten random samples of diary entries independently and then compared the results. To establish the intercoder reliability coefficient, the number of cases coded the same by the two authors was divided by the total number of cases coded by the authors (Scholfield, 1995). The intercoder reliability coefficient was 0.8. The authors resolved any coding discrepancies through discussion.

RESULTS AND DISCUSSION

"Would learner diaries help heighten students' metacognitive awareness of English learning over time?" Analysis of the students' diary entries throughout the course revealed that their metacognitive awareness of

EFL learning was clearly heightened. In the following report, the students' names are replaced by pseudonyms. The original sentences in the students' diaries are cited.

Person Knowledge

An examination of the diaries showed that the student-diarists became more aware of the cognitive processes underlying their learning. Most students reported changes in their understanding of their cognitive processes of listening, speaking and vocabulary learning. The early entries mentioned many serious difficulties (as perceived by the students) but these gradually became less problematic.

These Chinese EFL students seldom used English to communicate with one another before coming to Singapore. Thus, they encountered listening comprehension problems when they interacted with the local people, whose English was different from what they had heard over the radio or in the language classroom. Qiang believed that the local people he met spoke too fast (coded by the authors as cognitive factors that affect language learning), which was an obstacle to his listening comprehension. However, at the end of the course, he found that he could process the information better as he became more familiar with the local accent (nature of language and communication).

Qiang (Week 4):
... I asked a Singapore student... He told me what I should do. But he spoke very quickly and I couldn't understood him very well. So he repeated 2 or 3 times until I knew.

Qiang (Week 20):
Compared to speaking, I made more progress in listening. At the beginning of the course, .. I had to put all my attention in listening. But now I find it is very easy for me to follow my teachers and I began to get used to "Singlish".

Similar comments were made by other learners. At the beginning of the course, Gang mentioned in his diaries that he could only understand his teachers' English. Towards the end of the course, he found that he had made progress.

Certain individuals appeared to have been influenced by affective factors that affect learning, such as interest or the lack of interest, growing confidence, shyness and nervousness. In his diaries, Rong wrote:

> Rong (Week 1):
> I spoke less when I want to speak or have something to speak I didn't know how to say in English.

> Rong (Week 5):
> When I stayed with my classmates we never spoke English...they feel shy to speak English especially making some mistakes and smiled at by other persons.

Shyness was perhaps one of the main reasons why the students were quiet in class in the first few weeks. They had to overcome problems such as "talking with strangers" (Hua, Week 4) and anxiety about "being laughed at when I couldn't express myself correctly" (Jie, Week 8). Some students believed that it was strange for a Chinese to speak to another Chinese in English (Rong, Week 5). However, even when they were anxious, they encouraged themselves to persevere. The awareness of the above affective factors led them to use new strategies to solve the problems. Strategies like creating opportunities to converse with English-speaking people (Qin, Week 1; Dong, Week 2) and practising spoken English with friends in the students' hostels (Xin, Week 1; Yan, Week 1) were reported to be useful for skill improvement.

To overcome his shyness, Rong chose to practise his spoken English with his roommate because there was no one else. Once he got over the initial awkwardness, he could see the significance of the task:

> Rong (Week 7):
> I have spoke English with Gang in our room. ...we both want to improve our abilities of speaking. In our room, there are only us two. We didn't feel shy.

> Rong (Week 20):
> Now never shy when I speak English.

The above results show that the students' awareness of the cognitive and affective factors influencing them might have positive effects on their language learning. From the diary data, it would appear that these students were able to think about the problems and became more aware of their own information-processing styles and emotional responses. They then used appropriate strategies to overcome their weaknesses.

Strategic Knowledge

Students' knowledge about strategies increased over time. Many of them used different strategies to achieve their goals or to overcome their difficulties. For some, it was a trial-and-error approach. Others might have stumbled upon a strategy. In their first diary, all of them considered memorising new words to be the principal vocabulary learning strategy. When they were prompted to think about their language learning by the guidelines, some evaluated the strategic knowledge that they had acquired and started to gain new insights into the use of effective strategies.

For example, at the outset, Hao reported memorising new words as his strategy (strategy for particular tasks). He changed his approach when he had thought about how and why he should choose certain strategies (principles for strategy choice):

Hao (Week 1):
I should keep on reciting new words.

Hao (Week 2):
I don't know what I should pay more attention to? Comprehension, new words, gramma(sic), or sth. else?

Hao (Week 6):
I won't put the emphasis on new words. ...Because I find I can't memorise many words that I've noted down and plenty of words are not used frequently. I'll forget them soon.

Towards the end of the course, many students like Hao had a deeper knowledge about how to choose and use a strategy effectively. They began to realise that memorising words alone would not help them become more proficient. One possible reason is that diary-keeping had stimulated these students to rethink their strategy use. Their strategic knowledge developed rapidly as they moved from an EFL environment like China to a country such as Singapore, where English is widely used in daily life. They found that they should not only "learn" new words, but also "learn how to use" them. As Dong and Le wrote:

> Dong (Week 2):
> ...if we want to learn English better, we should put ourselves into an English language environment. That means you should talk more in English, think more in English and read more in English.

> Le (Week 3):
> I will master as more words as possible, not only know their meaning, but also understand how to use them.

The students tried out strategies like learning new words within a framework (Jian, Week 9) or reading local newspapers (Xin, Week 1). Their regular reflection upon their learning might have enabled them to become more aware of English learning and English usage, which helped them polish up their English vocabulary learning skills.

Task Knowledge

The diaries revealed a growing awareness of tasks, especially in the areas of speaking and listening, which were the major concerns for most students. In the first week of the course, the students were encouraged to listen to the radio after class. Although most of them reported listening to BBC World Service every day, few knew how to accomplish this listening task. After Qi had listened to BBC for two weeks, he assessed the level of difficulty of this task (task demand):

> Qi (Week 3):
> I haven't find any progress on my listening, and I am sure that in future I must make progress, I will listen to BBC everyday.

> Qi (Week 6):
> I only knew the word I heard, I didn't catch the whole sentence.

When he realised his weakness, Qi paid more attention to the listening task. He checked the meaning of an unfamiliar word and thought about the nature of English learning (nature of language and communication).

Qi (Week 12):
...learning English is not like learning mathematics. When you learn maths, you can say I know how to solve this problem, that problem, but to English you can't say so.

His hard work paid off finally. Two weeks later, he mentioned his progress in listening comprehension (task purpose or significance) and the guessing strategy he used to complete the task (strategies for particular task).

Qi (Week 14):
I can know the general meanings of BBC. Though I didn't understand it sometimes, I can make sure of what they talked about. According to my experience I can imagine what happened.

Some students like Qi might not have realised that they had acquired new task knowledge. As revealed in the second half of that week's diary, Qi reported that he could understand the coverage of a football match by BBC. Until he reported it in his diary, Qi did not know that the background knowledge he had acquired was useful to his listening comprehension (task demands):

Qi (Week 14):
Last night I listened to BBC. They talked about football. To my surprise, I found it was easy for me to understand what they said. And I understood all the words almost in half an hour. Maybe that's because I know something about the football.

From that week onwards, Qi had some idea about how to understand radio English and he had a clearer focus. The significance of the task (task purpose or significance) was reported in his last diary entry:

Qi (Week 20):
Now I can know what the English speaker said, I am sure that I have made some progress in English listening.

Similar comments were found in other students' diaries although the significance of the task varied from student to student. In his last diary entry, Ji wrote, "when I first listened to BBC, I could hardly catch anything. But now, I could understand BBC partially, sometimes completely!" (Ji, Week 20). The accomplishment of a task might have given the learners some encouragement, as Wu wrote, "I find that I have been able to catch several items of news from BBC. It makes me very happy" (Wu, Week 10).

The results of the above analysis suggest that when the students in this sample faced a problem during a task, they might not find the solutions immediately. Given time to reflect on their language learning after class, they might think about the nature of language learning as well as the factors that hindered the successful completion of the task. The authors speculate that the dynamic process of reflection might be one of the factors that contributed to the accomplishment of the task.

PEDAGOGICAL IMPLICATIONS

At the end of the course, the students were asked to evaluate the usefulness of diary-keeping in their English learning. Most of them reflected that they could see their learning processes through diaries. Some students suggested that they should try free-writing when they had a better command of English. However, to avoid writing diaries that are irrelevant to language learning, these students suggested that teachers give guidelines for the contents at the beginning but be more flexible about guidelines after a few weeks. Therefore, the authors recommend that from time to time teachers ask students to write on a particular topic of language learning. Topics like "How to increase my English vocabulary" or "How to overcome my shyness in speaking English" may stimulate students to reflect on and evaluate the metacognitive knowledge they have acquired.

To make full use of the learner diaries, teachers can initiate small group discussions regularly to guide students towards a greater awareness of metacognitive knowledge, clarify doubts and share experiences. During the discussion, teachers can introduce effective strategies to their students (Matsumoto, 1996), give students the opportunity to assess the effectiveness of their learner strategies (Goh, 1997), or encourage students to share their beliefs about language learning with others (Wenden, 1986). Exchange of ideas about the demands of a particular language task and ways to accomplish it may also enhance students' awareness of the language task. The results of this study support the arguments of Bailey (1983) and Matsumoto (1989) that affective factors determine the results of students' learning. Positive feedback from teachers on the diaries, to a certain extent, is an important motivating factor for students to be frank in their diary writing. Teachers' encouragement can carry students through difficult times. Teachers' advice on learning skills enables students to think about the tasks that they are doing. In addition, teachers can gauge the intangible affective factors involved in their students' language learning by reading and responding to the students' diaries.

CONCLUSION

In conclusion, learner diaries could be one of the tools that help Chinese students raise their metacognitive awareness of English learning over time. Moreover, learner diaries could be a valuable record of students' changing metacognitive awareness. However, since this study focused on a small group of Chinese EFL learners, the results of this study could not possibly be generalised for the population of all EFL learners. Therefore, the authors suggest that other teacher-researchers conduct similar diary studies with their own students. Besides, they could examine the effects of topical diary writing on their students' metacognitive awareness of language learning and compare the results with those of the present project.

REFERENCES

Bailey, K. M. (1983). Competitiveness and anxiety in adult second language learning: Looking at and through the diary studies. In H. W. Seliger & M. H. Long (Eds.), *Classroom-oriented Research in Second Language Acquisition* (pp. 67–103). Rowley, MA: Newbury House.

──────── (1990). The use of diary studies in teacher education programs. In J. C. Richards & D. Nunan (Eds.), *Second Language Teacher Education* (pp. 215–26). Cambridge: Cambridge University Press.

Chamot, A. U. & O'Malley, J. M. (1994). *The CALLA Handbook: Implementing the Cognitive Academic Language Learning Approach*. Addison-Wesley Publishing Company.

Ellis, G. & Sinclair, B. (1989). *Learning to Learn English: A Course in Learner Training*. Cambridge: Cambridge University Press.

Goh, C. (1997). Metacognitiveawareness and second language listeners. *ELT Journal*, 51(4): 361–69.

Matsumoto, K. (1989). An analysis of a Japanese ESL learner's diary: Factors involved in the L2 learning process. *JALT Journal*, 11(2): 167–92.

_____ (1996). Helping L2 learners reflect on classroom learning. *ELT Journal*, 50(2): 143–49.

Nunan, D. (1988). *The Learner-centered Curriculum*. Cambridge: Cambridge University Press.

_____ (1996). Learner strategy training in the classroom: An action research study. *TESOL Journal*, 6: 35–41.

Scholfield, P. (1995). *Quantifying Language: A Researcher's and Teacher's Guide to Gathering Language Data and Reducing it to Figures*. Clevedon, Avon, England: Multilingual Matters Ltd.

Wenden, A. L. (1986). Helping language learners think about learning. *ELT Journal*, 40(1): 3–12.

_____ (1991). *Learner Strategies for Learner Autonomy*. Prentice-Hall International.

_____ (1995). Learner training in context: A knowledge-based approach. *System*, 23(2): 183–94.

APPENDIX A. THE METACOGNITIVE KNOWLEDGE CLASSIFICATION SCHEME DEVELOPED FOR THE PRESENT STUDY

Type	Category	Definition	Example*
Person Knowledge	Cognitive factors that affect learning	Knowledge of the cognitive aspects that influence the perception, organisation and recall of information	Some films can be understood easily but some others are different...because the actors always keep on speaking... They also speak so fast that I often cannot catch it (Wang, Week 15).
	Affective factors that affect learning	Knowledge of the emotional dimensions that influence language learning	I am afraid to open my mouth to speak English because I don't want to make mistakes (Gang, Week 1).
Strategic Knowledge	Strategies for particular tasks	Learners' knowledge of strategies that they have used	My basic strategy is to skip all the unknown words and to seek for the topic I'm interested in, then read through know about its basic meaning (Dong, Week 13).
	Principles for strategy choice	Learners' knowledge concerning why they used a strategy to increase their language proficiency	I began to read more newspaper...it would be good not only to enlarge my vocabulary, but also improve my ability of writing (Cheng, Week 9).
	Evaluation of strategy use	Learners' assessment of a strategy that they have tried	I usually looked up every new word in the dictionary... But since this week I felt that it was not very useful (Yu, Week 3).
	Possible strategies for improving skills	Learners' knowledge about the strategies that they will probably use to improve their language skills	Next week I will go to Computer Centre to email my friends in China. So I can do more writing in English (Jing, Week 3).

(cont'd overleaf)

APPENDIX A. *(cont'd)*

Type	Category	Definition	Example*
Task Knowledge	Task purpose or significance	Learners' knowledge relating to why they do a task and how they appreciate its significance	I think the most useful thing I've learned this week is writing skills. Through this, I acquire the knowledge 'how to chose a thesis' (Wei, Week 2).
	Nature of language and communication	Knowledge of how language is used in interaction, including the differences among cultures and genres	There are only 1500 basic words in Chinese. You can tell the meaning of a phrase by connecting the meaning of each word. But you can't do that in English (Xiao, Week 2).
	Need for deliberate effort	Knowledge regarding when conscious effort is required in the accomplishment of a particular task	I cannot cover a new word naturally…so I think I should improve my skill of it in the following days (Wen, Week 6).
	Task demands	Knowledge associated with how to complete a task, and what resources are needed to perform the task	Since we have learned some knowledge in class, it's a little easier for me to talk about this topic (Qiang, Week 8).

Note: * The diary extracts are cited in their original form. Students' names are replaced with pseudonyms.
Source: Adapted from Wenden (1991: 49).

CHAPTER 3

The Use of Learner Diaries in the Teaching of English as a Second Language

JESSIE TENG SZE MEI

BACKGROUND OF STUDY

When I was a student, both my English and Chinese language teachers recommended diary writing as an effective means of improving language proficiency. However, these diaries were meant to be private and read only by the writers themselves. In recent years, learner diaries have taken on the additional role of being used as instruments in language learning research, where either the diarist or another person analyses the diary for various factors affecting language learning.

The aim of this chapter is to describe how I implemented the writing of a diary as part of my teaching strategy, what I learnt about language learning from my students' diaries, and how these discoveries have helped me to be more effective pedagogically.

REVIEW OF DIARY STUDIES

The study of diaries (or journals) has been popular amongst researchers who seek in-depth information about the personal learning experiences of language learners. For example, Parkinson and Howell-Richardson (1990) administered structural diaries to guide learner participants in their research towards reflection on a number of factors under investigation, while Polanyi (1995) sought to discover what was learnt by language learners during foreign language study abroad. Diaries have also been used to investigate a range of language learning-related issues, such as perceptions of language learners and the social aspects of language learning. For example, Miller and Ginsberg (1995) studied the theories students had of the nature of language while Maguire and Graves (2001) explored the relationship between L2 learning and identity construction using ESL learners' journal writing. In addition, journals have also proven useful as tools for reflection and introspection for the diarists themselves (Lowe, 1987; Campbell, 1996). Several of these diarists are in fact sophisticated researcher-language learners (Schumann and Schumann, 1977; Bailey, 1983; Schmidt and Frota, 1986; Cummings, 1996) whose diary studies have contributed much to the understanding of second/foreign language learning from the learner's point of view. In addition, diaries have also been kept by language learners (Parkinson and Howell-Richardson, 1990; Tsui, 1996), inexperienced trainee (pre-service) teachers (Jarvis, 1992), as well as in-service teachers (Lowe, 1987; Richards, 1992), who have benefited from being able to use their diaries to reflect on their learning/ teaching.

Bailey (1983) noted that diary studies have several advantages, including providing developmental data such as tracing attitudinal changes through sequential entries, revealing diversity among learners even within an apparently homogenous class, and enabling researchers and learners to document and counteract factors which are detrimental to the learner's language learning.

Possibly one of the most significant features of diary studies in educational research is that they "allow us to see the classroom experience as a dynamic and complex process through the eyes of a language learner" (Bailey, 1983:98). Similarly, in the study of language learning, the language learner diary can be employed to "invite careful reflection in the language learning process in order to bring key features into prominence" (Richards, 1992:144). In fact, recent works on teaching and research methodologies for English language teachers, such as McDonough and McDonough (1997), Richards (1998), Burns (1999) and Bailey (2001), include references to the use of diaries and discussions on their merits and limitations for research and in English language teaching/learning.

Language learning diaries and learner diaries have been differentiated from normal diaries in that the contents of the former are centred on the learning experiences of the (language) learner and exclude content which are seemingly not relevant to (language) learning. However, my use of "learner diary" in this context simply refers to "the diary of the learner", which may (and often does) include records of much apparently non-

(language) learning-related content, such as the writer's feelings of homesickness.

Finally, diary studies (Schumann and Schumann, 1977; Schumann, 1980; Bailey, 1980, 1983; Lowe, 1987; Richards, 1992; Hilleson, 1996; Peck, 1996) have also revealed a wide range of affective and environmental factors not previously highlighted by other studies on foreign language learning. Such factors include the influence of anxiety in language learning and the importance of being adjusted to new (especially foreign) surroundings.

RESEARCH PARTICIPANTS AND METHODOLOGY

Since the early 1990s, the Singapore Ministry of Education has been offering undergraduate scholarships to PRC (People's Republic of China) students to study in either of the first two local universities in Singapore, the National University of Singapore and the Nanyang Technological University. These students were mostly undergraduates in their first semester in Chinese local universities. They were referred to as SM3 (Senior Middle 3) students.

The students whose diaries are examined in this chapter were part of the sixth cohort of SM3 PRC scholars who underwent a six-month intensive English proficiency course from December 1997 to June 1998 at the Centre for English Language Communication of the National University of Singapore. This was to prepare them for their undergraduate studies in the local universities, where English is the primary language medium of education.

The experimental group comprised 19 students — 15 boys and 4 girls aged between 18 and 20. They attended 52 hours of English lessons a week from Mondays to Fridays. I met them every Tuesday. I introduced the learner diary assignment in my second lesson, and the activity continued for five months. The following guidelines were given for writing their diaries:

• Their diaries would not be graded but the activity was compulsory (cf study by Allison, 1998 in which diaries were not assessed formally but which made up a component of an existing assessed heading of "active course participation"). This was to encourage students to write without the fear of being penalised for language errors in their diaries.

- They could write in their English diary as often as they wanted, but they had to submit their diaries every alternate week for me to read and respond to. This was because they would hand in their diaries one week, and I would return their diaries the next week with my responses.
- As the diary was also a channel of communication between the diarist and me, I encouraged them to ask me questions in their diaries.
- There was no word limit but I encouraged them to write at least a paragraph, not only one or two sentences, per entry.
- They were not restricted in what they were to write about, though I emphasised I would be interested in anything related to their language learning.
- They could submit hard copies of their diaries or send them through electronic mail (email).

At the end of the course, I obtained 13 students' diaries as data for analysis. I was not able to obtain all the students' diaries as some of these had been misplaced, having been written on loose sheets of writing pad paper. As the data collected were meant for qualitative, and not quantitative, analysis, it was perhaps not crucial to have all the students' diaries.

RESEARCH FINDINGS: ANALYSIS OF LEARNER DIARIES

The diaries afforded me, the teacher, a behind-the-scenes insight into the diarists' lives, beliefs, attitudes and experiences. Most diaries contained narrative accounts of events, descriptions of places or people that had left an impression on the diarists. I had hoped that the learner diaries would be an alternative channel of communication between the students and me, but this type of continuous exchange on paper was only successful with one student and the 'conversation' was centred mostly on one topic. It is not clear why the mutual exchange I had hoped for through the diaries was unsuccessful with the other students. It could be because they did not perceive the diary as performing that function, they did not have the habit of reading and responding to my input, or they did not see the need to carry on such exchanges in the diary.

However, the two most significant aspects of the learner diary for me are its language and content, as these provided me with information that directly helped me to be more effective both as their language teacher and as a teacher in general.

Language of the Learner Diary

The language produced by the students enabled me to better assess their language proficiency, particularly their writing skills, in the areas of grammar and vocabulary. In terms of grammar, I could identify common errors in the use of articles, tenses and prepositions. Common errors in the spelling of particular words were also easily spotted.

In terms of vocabulary, I could assess each student's range of active vocabulary with respect to his/her use of words, idioms and proverbs. The diaries also helped me in becoming more aware of common errors in the use of certain words, whether these errors were idiosyncratic or common to the group.

For example, many students were unable to differentiate the difference in usage and meaning between the words 'wish' and 'hope'. This is probably because in their mother tongue, Chinese, there is one expression for both meanings. The students thus confuse 'wish' and 'hope'. In fact, they tend to use 'hope' in its noun form while 'wish' is more frequently used in its verb form. Hence, it is common to find students using the verb 'wish' instead of the verb 'hope' in sentences like "I wish I can get on well with other people of other races in Singapore" and "I wish that I won't forget to return it to you the next Tuesday."

A second example is the apparent confusion of some students between the use of 'come' and 'go'. They appeared to be writing from the perspective of still being in China instead of actually being in Singapore. For example, one student wrote, "As I read the letter (from her friends in China), I seem to come back to Shandong University."

In addition to being able to diagnose the individual grammatical and writing problems faced by students, the diaries allowed me to see trends in the students' mistakes. These errors include the use of phrases, such as colloquial phrases translated directly from their mother tongue, they would not otherwise have used in normal academic writing. For example, a student wrote of her visit to a beach, "All kinds of beautiful words were filled in my chest." Another student wrote, "I called my father for some words. The phone took me S$2.5."(*sic*) These examples showed that the students were actively translating from their mother tongue instead of thinking in English.

Content of the Learner Diaries

The content of the diaries revealed information concerning the students'
language learning experiences and difficulties, as well as affective and
environmental factors affecting their language learning. It also reflected
various personal aspects of the diarists, such as their beliefs, attitudes and
personalities.

Language Learning

The content of the diaries covered a range of topics in the area of language
learning. Therefore, I was able to gain a deeper and wider understanding
of four key aspects in the language learning of my students: their language
learning strategies, their beliefs about language learning, their perceived
needs for university study, and their responses to various class activities.

Language learning strategies

One key topic was the language learning strategies employed by the
students, mostly outside of class. The diaries frequently recorded what the
students did to improve their English, such as listening to the British
Broadcasting Corporation or the Voice of America on radio. In conjunction,
the diaries often also described difficulties the diarists encountered when
implementing such strategies, such as not being able to catch what the
broadcaster said because the pace was too fast. Furthermore, the diarists
also revealed the difficulties they faced in their general language learning
experiences. For instance, a concern that was often expressed was how
they could not remember the great number of new words they came across
each day in their lessons.

Beliefs about language learning

I came to better understand my students' beliefs about language learning
as they would occasionally reveal their feelings and opinions regarding
language learning. For example, some students felt increasing their
vocabulary bank was very important. Their diaries did not specify which
kinds of vocabulary they felt they needed to acquire or had difficulty
doing so. Their problem appeared to be more of a quantitative one, for
several of them expressed their limited vocabulary and the need to
enlarge it.

One student wrote, "It's very hard for me to enter this English world freely. Vocabulary is the first and biggest enemy we now face." The pressure and frustration of trying to learn new words is expressed by another student who wrote, "In listening and reading, I find that there are a lot of new words I don't know. That's to say, my vocabulary is too limited. I want to increase my vocabulary but when I learn a new word by heart, I often find that I'll forget it soon! Now please tell me how I can increase my vocabulary and in what way I can remember new words." A third student wrote clearly about her beliefs in how best to address her problem:

> I think there are two problems I must solve presently. The first problem is what I should do if I want a large vocabulary. Some suggested that I recite some new words from a handbook every day. Some suggested that it would be better if I looked up the new words in the dictionary while reading. But I think neither of them is suitable for me. I think the best way to remember new words is to only read an article first, not looking up the new words and only guessing the meanings of them by the contexts, then look them up in the dictionary to see whether the guessed meanings are wrong or right. In this way, I can remember the new words easily.

Grabe (1991) noted the importance of vocabulary in fluent reading while more recent works (e.g., Cobb and Horst, 2001; Coxhead and Nation, 2001) recommend strategies training in vocabulary development for academic reading.

Perceived needs for university study

The diaries showed me what language skills the students thought were needed for university study. For example, several asked how they could improve their reading skills as they were aware they would have a lot to read during their undergraduate study. They were particularly concerned about speed-reading as they were afraid they would not read fast enough to cover all they would be required to study. In response to this concern, I raised the issue in class and asked for suggestions for solving this problem. Some students felt this problem would be reduced if they had a larger vocabulary, as this would reduce the need to check up unfamiliar vocabulary in the dictionary. Others suggested applying the reading skills of skimming and scanning (which we had covered in the course weeks before). I added that it would often not be necessary to read every word of every textbook, and that they should look out for relevant information. One way they could do this was by referring to the content and index pages of the book to locate the information they needed.

Responses to class activities

I was given an insight into how they felt about various class activities conducted by myself or other tutors. Some of these students were honest enough to give negative feedback on some activities, although they were too polite to give negative comments about my lessons. However, they did provide some suggestions for improvement or for other activities they would like me to conduct. For example, one student wrote, "We've got relatively adequate chances to practise orally. But it is critical to direct us how to organise our ideas in a proper way in speaking." On listening activities, another student suggested, "We should be given more tapes to listen to and have some native speaker give us talks."

Affective Factors

Some diary studies have shown the importance of affective factors in the language learning experience. These factors have included nesting patterns — the need to build a suitable home in the foreign country — and transition anxiety — anxiety caused by travel to a foreign country to stay there (Schumann and Schumann, 1977); responses to physical and social environments (Bailey, 1980); competitiveness and anxiety, particularly anxiety related to oral language production (Bailey, 1983); motivation, group cohesion and preference for a particular physical position in the classroom (Lowe, 1987); cultural factors and the importance of authenticity in communicative activities (Richards, 1992). In the same way, my students' diaries have also revealed various aspects of their personalities and interests. These topics can be grouped into five categories: students' areas of interests, students' general beliefs and attitudes, amusing anecdotes of students' experiences, students' family backgrounds and personal & sensitive issues.

Students' areas of interests

This category includes the students' hobbies (such as reading, listening to music and swimming) and their interests (in areas such as politics, sports and culture). Knowing the students' interests enabled me to use examples relevant to them in my teaching. This, in turn, helped me to gain and maintain their attention during lessons. Knowing my students' interests also gave me ideas for writing and discussion topics. For example, many of them wrote about how new and different everything was for them in Singapore. So I decided to give them an assignment comparing the differences between China and Singapore.

Students' general beliefs and attitudes

The beliefs I refer to here include their political viewpoints (and some have very strong political viewpoints) as well as their philosophies of life and worldview. For example, one student expressed unhappiness at what a teacher at his hostel had said,

> In yesterday's game one teacher asked us PRC students, "What will Taiwan government do with you if you enter Taiwan?" of course we can't go to Taiwan freely and Taiwanese can't go to China mainland freely, but Taiwan is territory of China, this is a fact and can't be changed. I didn't think this political question should be put out at that time.

These beliefs often affect their attitudes to various issues and towards other people. Therefore, having a better understanding of these basic beliefs, especially in the areas of politics and religion, helped me to be more sensitive and tactful when addressing these issues when they came up for discussion during the lessons.

Amusing anecdotes of students' daily life experiences

Reading about such experiences helped me know more about what was going on in each student's life, which helped me understand the student better as a whole. Furthermore, when appropriate, I encouraged the student to share the experience in class in order that the others could benefit from it. For example, I had encouraged the students to gain more exposure to the English language, and suggested one way to do that was to listen to English songs. One student later wrote of how being forced to listen to English songs gave him an opportunity to develop a liking for them.

> Friday afternoon is always lovely to students. After finishing all week lessons, we went back to the hostel. We took out music tapes and want to relax ourselves in pop songs. But there was only one (tape)

recorder in the room, we had at least a dozen tapes in all. Though, I insisted we should listen (to) Chinese songs, which I often do before, the other three roommate persist English songs. Obeying the majority, I unwillingly listen to English song. It was not long before I realized that some English songs were very sound (pleasant to listen to) as well. Though sometimes I couldn't get the lyric, I thought I would make more contacts with English song than before.

Students' family backgrounds

Families become especially important to the students as many of them had never been away from home before. Even the most independent students confessed to homesickness and a new appreciation of their families. Thus, their diaries often mentioned their parents and siblings. These records helped me to respond by way of writing and/or talking to individual students about their families in order to provide emotional support. For example, one student wrote about receiving news that his father had given up smoking. He was happy because his father's 25-year smoking habit had adversely affected his health. The student went on to reminisce how strong his father used to be, and expressed sadness at how old he had now become. He wrote,

> He was always the champion of the 100 metre dash of the school he taught in. When I was young I was very weak and "small". I always did bad in P.E. ...But one day, I found that I can run very fast and my strength is very big...Now, I can run faster than my father and my strength is bigger than his. But I really know it is not because I'm growing up but Father is growing old. Father is really no longer a young man. But I'm now a young man. But I don't know why Father is so happy while I'm so upset ... Today, I heard Father's voice on the line again. Judged from his voice, he is not very well. After all, he smoked for so many years...It can really make me cry!

It surprised me that this usually tough-looking student had such emotional concerns. I wrote back in his diary,

> It's great that your father has finally stopped smoking! I know what it's like to see your parents grow old... But your father is happy to see you grow into a fine, strong young man with lots of potential. When a person is young, he/she lives for his/her own dreams. But when he/she grows old, he/she finds delight in his/

her children's dreams and achievements. That's why it's important for us to fulfil our responsibilities to our parents by becoming the best that we can be.

Personal and sensitive issues

As I built up rapport with the students, they became more open in sharing their thoughts and feelings with me. As I often talked about various issues openly, including issues which had been "forbidden" in their previous schools and university such as political issues and issues related to romantic relationships between the opposite sexes, the students sometimes asked me questions related to such issues in their diaries. Their common themes of interest were interpersonal relationships (particularly boy-girl relationships), their future (careers and families), religion and politics. I found that the female students asked more questions about going steady, and were more willing to share their personal experiences and feelings with me.

I believe such exchanges through the diaries not only helped to build rapport and deepen understanding between individual students and me, but also increased their trust in, and respect for, me both as their teacher and their friend. This was translated into positive responses to me in class. Hence, communicating about personal and sensitive issues with the students through their diaries indirectly helped to establish a more responsive and attentive classroom atmosphere.

In addition, having better rapport with my students and deeper understanding of their thoughts and attitudes gave me a glimpse of their perspectives. This, in turn, helped me to motivate them. For example, there were times when the students invariably would feel tired of attending English classes every day, and would appear listless and distracted in class. Knowing that one of their reasons for doing well was to do their parents proud, I would encourage them to envisage their graduation day, and how proud their parents would be of them, reminding them that it was important to get a good foundation in their English in order to do well in their studies. Such pep talks seemed to provide at least a small boost to their flagging energy from time to time throughout the six-month course.

Environmental Factors

The diaries also recorded various environmental or external factors which affected the students' language learning in one way or another.

These factors included what the students did with their time, for example, going to the Media Resource Library to watch English movies during lunch time and attending free English tuition provided by religious groups; the influence of peers on learning English, for example, a student was hampered in his attempt to practise his oral English because his friends found it awkward to speak to him in English; and events that motivated the students to learn English, such as being able to communicate with a Malay bus-driver in English.

Having an idea about these factors helped me understand what was helping or hindering my students' language learning, so that I could advise them on how to create a more conducive environment for their language learning outside of class. For example, knowing that students felt awkward communicating with each other in English outside of class, I gave them an out-of-class assignment. I had the class divided into small groups of threes or fours, and instructed them to meet each other for half an hour every night, till the end of the course, to speak to each other in English. Knowing that it was an assignment lessened the awkwardness for them. So even though this assignment was not assessed (and there was no way for me to find out if they actually did it), it gave them impetus to practise their oral skills outside of class time, and many of them did carry out the task for at least some weeks. One enthusiastic group continued the practice for a few months, while the others stopped, possibly because they grew tired of it or became lazy, or because they were too busy to meet as homework piled up towards the latter part of the course.

FEEDBACK FROM LEARNERS

In addition to analysing the diaries, I was interested in the students' response to the activity of diary writing as a whole. At the end of the course, I developed and distributed a feedback form to the class (Appendix A shows the questions which elicited feedback on writing diaries). The students were given the forms to fill. Out of 19 students, 9 students returned their forms.

When asked to rank the level of usefulness of *Writing diary* according to a Likert scale of 1–5 (1 being "Not useful" and 5 being "Very useful"), all the respondents ranked the activity as 4 – "Quite useful" (6 respondents) — or 5 – "Very useful" (3 respondents). In terms of level of enjoyment with ranking on a similar scale, five of the respondents ranked the activity 3 ("Enjoyed some") and four ranked it 4 ("Quite enjoyed").

All nine students listed *Writing diary* as one of the activities which helped in improving their writing skills, while three listed it as helpful in improving their vocabulary and five listed it as helpful in improving their grammar.

Two indicated that they thought we should have had more of the activity while another two preferred less of it. As the feedback forms are anonymous, I could not find out the reasons for this indication. However, verbal feedback received from some students about writing their diaries indicate that the preference for less of the activity may be because they felt they had nothing to write in their diaries or because they felt it added to their workload.

As the number of respondents is fairly small, this feedback can only serve as an indication of the reactions of the respondents rather than of all the students, and is therefore limited in its generalisability. Nevertheless, it is a reflection that at least some language learners who engage in this activity are likely to respond positively to it.

IMPLICATIONS OF FINDINGS

The learner feedback shows that writing diaries is an activity which is both possible for and welcomed by foreign language students. The findings have revealed advantages of using learner diaries in the language classroom for both learners and teachers.

One advantage of learner diaries is that they allow the students to initiate topics and write on whatever they wish. This can motivate the students to write more extensively as the topics are of interest to them. In this way, the diaries also often reveal the students' personal feelings, various kinds of experiences, including their language learning experiences, and what is important to them. Sometimes, the students also reveal something of their family background, character and personality. All this information helps me as their teacher to better understand the students and their individual needs. It also enables me to pay attention to the individual by giving specific advice in the diaries, such as giving ideas on how to increase vocabulary to one student while providing suggestions on how to improve speaking skills to another. In giving such advice, I also take into consideration the student's personality and character, so as to suggest language learning strategies which I felt they would be comfortable with.

For example, a common question asked by students was how to improve their speaking skills. Although I suggested various strategies to the class as a whole, I tended to emphasise various strategies to different individuals in their diaries when they asked for the same advice. To a student who was visibly shy, I encouraged her to practise speaking English into a tape recorder and listening to her own speech until she had the confidence to speak more often to others. To another student who was outgoing and obviously good at socialising, I suggested that he find opportunities to speak English with not only his friends but also those he did not know. One way he could do that was to pretend to ask strangers on the street for information such as the time or directions to a certain place.

As a result of the students being able to write on their topics of interests in their diaries, I was also able to tap on those topics as a source of ideas for language learning activities, such as essays, debates and project work.

A second advantage is that the diaries enable the students to express their thoughts via a non-threatening channel. This enables the teacher to enter the inner thoughts of students who are shy or who speak little due to poor speaking skills. One student often gave monosyllabic answers when I conversed with him but he proved to be relatively "fluent" in his writing. This made me realise his silence was not due to a lack of vocabulary, but because he was shy. So I tried to get him to speak more often in class by directing questions at him, and by speaking to him during breaks or before class started. Eventually, he seemed less withdrawn in class and started participating more actively in group discussions, and even occasionally volunteered his views in class discussions.

Another advantage of writing a diary is that it encourages the students to ask various kinds of language-related and language learning questions, especially since the teacher does not have enough time to answer those questions in class.

Lastly, in terms of language, writing diaries provides the students practice in (mostly) narrative and descriptive writing. At the same time, the writing enables the teacher not only to diagnose problems each student has in the language or in language learning, but also to note common language errors (such as the misuse of certain words) or language learning problems (such as difficulty in speaking) faced by the students. These areas can then be addressed in class or with individual students, whichever is more appropriate. Several students brought up the difficulty of learning new vocabulary effectively, and thus I discussed different strategies which they could employ to help in increasing their vocabulary.

LIMITATIONS OF DIARY WRITING IN TEACHING

Although learner diaries can be useful to the language teacher, it has certain limitations in its application as a teaching tool. These are mainly due to the 'informal' nature of the activity in that there are relatively few restrictions compared to other writing assignments like essay or summary writing, which is usually limited in the scope of the content and the length. Therefore, advantages of the activity, such as students' freedom to initiate any topic, may also become limitations.

Without specifying topics for students' diaries, the teacher also has less control over the kind of language and content that s/he wishes to elicit from them. Of course the teacher may, from time to time, limit the scope of diary entries by specifying what students should write on. For example, I wanted to find out the difficulties they had with a summary assignment they had been given, so I requested that they write, in their diaries, about the difficulties they had as they did the assignment. However, if the teacher too frequently determines what is to be written in the diaries, student initiative may be stifled.

The second limitation lies in the type of writing that is mostly generated in diary writing. As most diary accounts centre on what the diarists feel or have experienced, they tend to engage largely in descriptive and narrative writing. Occasionally, however, a student may use the opportunity to express his/her views on certain matters, thus producing writing of an argumentative or analytical nature. One such student of mine wrote mini-essays expressing his views on a variety of issues ranging from environmental conservation to the effectiveness of Singapore fines for different offences.

The most serious limitation is the lack of methods to assess students' responses to the teacher's suggestions, although brief acknowledgements are sometimes offered. For example, one student wrote in reply to my exhortation to do well and become famous, like some of his other countrymen, "Thank you for your encouragement. I think I can hardly be one of them. But I'll try my best." In general, it is difficult to evaluate the impact and effectiveness of advice given to students in the diaries as diarists seldom provide feedback on teacher responses to their diary entries.

Due to the lack of control over content, length and types of writing, diary writing is perhaps best used as a supplementary activity. Moreover, since information that benefits the teacher tends to emerge over time, it should be an ongoing activity instead of a one-time assignment.

CONCLUSION

The practice of writing learner diaries has benefits for both language learners and teachers. Not only did the students in my class find the activity useful in improving their target language, but as their teacher, I was able to be more effective in my teaching as a result of what I learnt from their diaries. Although it has its limitations, it is nevertheless helpful to both teachers and students, and therefore, I highly recommend it to language teachers, especially those teaching language proficiency courses to foreign students.

REFERENCES

Allison, D. (1998). Investigating learners' course diaries as explorations of language. *Language Teaching Research*, 2(1): 24–47.

Bailey, K. M. (1980). An introspective analysis of an individual's language learning experience. In S. D. Krashen and R. C. Scarcella (Eds.), *Research in SLA* (pp. 58–65). Rowley, Massachussetts: Newbury House.

_____ (1983). Competitiveness and anxiety in adult second language learning: Looking at and through the diary studies. In H. W. Seliger and M. H. Long (Eds.), *Classroom Oriented Research in Second Language Acquisition* (pp. 67–103). Rowley, Massachussetts: Newbury House.

_____ (2001). Action research, teacher research and classroom research in language teaching. In M. Celce–Murcia (Ed.), *Teaching English as a Second or Foreign Language* (3rd ed.) (pp. 489–98). Boston: Heinle & Heinle.

Bailey, K. M. & Nunan, D. (Eds.) (1996). *Voices from the Language Classroom: Qualitative Research in Second Language Education*. Cambridge: Cambridge University Press.

Burns, A. (1999). *Collaborative Action Research for English Language Teachers*. Cambridge: Cambridge University Press.

Campbell, C. (1996). Socialising with the teachers and prior language learning experience: A diary study. In K. M. Bailey and D. Nunan (Eds.), *Voices from the Language Classroom: Qualitative Research in Second Language Education* (pp. 201–223). Cambridge: Cambridge University Press.

Cobb, T. & Horst, M. (2001). Reading academic English: Carrying learners across the lexical threshold. In J. Flowerdew and M. Peacock (Eds.), *Research Perspectives on English for Academic Purposes* (pp. 315–29). Cambridge: Cambridge University Pres.

Coxhead, A. & Nation, P. (2001). The specialised vocabulary of English for academic purposes. In J. Flowerdew and M. Peacock (Eds.), (pp. 252–67).

Cummings, M. C. (1996). Sardo revisited: Voice, faith, and multiple repeaters. In K. M. Bailey and D. Nunan (Eds.), (pp. 224–35).

Flowerdew, J. & Peacock, M. (Eds.) (2001). *Research Perspectives on English for Academic Purposes.* Cambridge: Cambridge University Press.

Freed, B. F. (Ed.) (1995). *Second Language Acquisition in a Study Abroad Context.* Philadelphia, PA: John Benjamins B.V.

Grabe, W. (1991). Current developments in second language reading research. *TESOL Quarterly,* 25(3): 375–406.

Hilleson, M. (1996). I want to talk with them, but I don't want them to hear. In K. M. Bailey and D. Nunan (Eds.), (pp. 248–75).

Jarvis, J. (1992). Using diaries for teacher reflection on in–service courses. *English Language Teaching Journal,* 46 (2): 133–43.

Lowe, T. (1987). An experiment in role reversal: Teachers as language learners. *English Language Teaching Journal,* 41 (2): 89–96.

Parkinson, B. & Howell-Richardson, C. (1990). Learner diaries. In C. Brumfit and R. Mitchell, *Research in the Language Classroom* (pp. 128–40). ELT Documents 133: British Council.

McDonough, J. & McDonough, S. (1997). *Research Methods for English Language Teachers.* London; New York: St. Martins Press.

Miller, L. & Ginsberg, R. B. (1995). Folklinguistic theories on language learning. In B.F. Freed (Ed.), (pp. 293–315).

Peck, S. (1996). Language learning diaries as mirrors of students' cultural sensitivity. In K. M. Bailey and D. Nunan (Eds.), (pp. 236–47).

Polanyi, L. (1995). Language learning and living abroad: Stories from the field. In B. F. Freed (Ed.), (pp. 271–91).

Richards, J. C. (1998). *Beyond Training: Perspectives on Language Teacher Education.* Cambridge; New York: Cambridge University Press.

Richards, K. (1992). Pepys into a TEFL course. *English Language Teaching Journal,* 46 (2): 145–52.

Maguire, M. H. & Graves, B. (2001). Speaking personalities in primary school children's L2 writing. *TESOL Quarterly,* 35(4): 561–93.

Schmidt, R. W. & Frota, S. N. (1986). Developing basic conversational ability in a second language: A case study of an adult learner of Portuguese. In R. D. Richard (Ed.), *Talking To Learn: Conversation in Second Language Acquisition* (pp. 237–326). Rowley, Massachussetts: Newbury House.

Schumann, F. and Schumann, J. (1977). Diary of a language learner. In H. D. Brown et al. (Eds.), *On TESOL '77, Teaching and Learning English as a Second Language: Trends in Research and Practice.* Washington: TESOL.

Tsui, A. B. M. (1996). Reticence and anxiety in second language learning. In K. M. Bailey and D. Nunan (Eds.), (pp. 145–67).

APPENDIX A.   SM3 FEEDBACK FORM

Please fill in the boxes with the appropriate number as given:

Very useful – 5   Quite useful – 4   Somewhat useful – 3   A little useful – 2
Not useful – 1

Enjoyed a lot – 5   Quite enjoyed – 4   Enjoyed some – 3   Enjoyed a little – 2
Did not enjoy – 1

No.	Activity	Level of Usefulness	Level of Enjoyment
1.	Writing Diary		
2.	Learning & Teaching Songs		
3.	Language Games		
4.	Giving Short Talks		
5.	Guest Speakers		
6.	Impromptu 1-Minute Talks		
7.	Writing Letters to Secret Friend		
8.	Oral Presentations		
9.	Error Correction		
10.	Essays		
11.	Reading Short Articles		
12.	Debates		

1.   Which activities (write the numbers) helped in improving your

   (a) Listening skills : _____

   (b) Speaking skills : _____

   (c) Reading skills   : _____

   (d) Writing skills   : _____

   (e) Vocabulary   : _____

   (f) Grammar   : _____

2.   Which activities should we have more of (write the numbers)? _____

3.   Which activities should we have less of (write the numbers)? _____

4. What other activities can you suggest for improving

   (a) Listening skills : _____

   (b) Speaking skills : _____

   (c) Reading skills : _____

   (d) Writing skills : _____

   (e) Vocabulary : _____

   (f) Grammar : _____

5. Was there an activity/ activities which you found especially useful? If yes, which one(s) and why?

6. Was there an activity/ activities which you did not find useful at all? If yes, which one(s) and why?

7. Please feel free to give any other feedback.

CHAPTER 4

Reflections of ESL and EFL Students Through Email: An Exploratory Study

HAPPY GOH & TAN KIM LUAN

INTRODUCTION

As English language teachers we are always asking ourselves how best we can help our students learn the target language more effectively. We wonder if the activities in class have been beneficial to all; we wonder if what was taught has been learnt by all. We have observed that some students are able to progress faster than others, while some others struggle to improve their English proficiency. We wanted to find out why this is so.

One of the ways to enable teachers to become aware of the learning needs and difficulties of individual students is to ask students to keep a journal or diary. This will provide a channel for students to give feedback to teachers, not only of their difficulties but also their opinions of class lessons. By analysing and evaluating their learning, students are actively participating in the learning process. In fact, studies on learner strategies, learner beliefs, attitudes and perceptions (O'Malley and Chamot, 1990; Oxford, 1990; Wenden, 1991; Wenden and Rubin, 1987) have shown that when language learners think about their language learning, they can benefit from their reflections. Teachers too can obtain insights about effective and ineffective strategies, and the difficulties they face in completing the assigned tasks. They can modify their teaching methods to meet the needs of the students. In this way, a learner-centred approach is adopted.

In order to investigate these learner strategies, learner beliefs, attitudes and perceptions, and other areas such as learner anxiety and cultural issues, language learning diaries are used. There are basically two types of language learning diary studies (Bailey, 1991). The first involves the researcher who is also the diarist while the second is the researcher analysing the diaries written by other language learners. Matsumoto (1989) has called the first type "introspective" diary studies and the second type "non-introspective" studies.

The first published analysis of the "non-introspective" type is Bailey and Ochsner's (1983) work on competitiveness and anxiety in adult second language learners. In another investigation, Matsumoto (1989) analysed the diary of a 19-year-old Japanese girl who reflected upon her language learning experience in an intensive English course in the United States. In some studies, in addition to the diaries, qualitative investigations such as questionnaires, structured reviews and classroom observations were used (Matsumoto, 1996).

According to Bailey and Ochsner (1983: 189), "a diary study in second language learning, acquisition or teaching is an account of a second language experience as recorded in a first person journal". The diarist thus writes about "affective factors, language learning strategies, and his own perceptions". Of course the scope of what could be written in the diary can be narrowed depending on the purpose of the diarist or researcher. One kind of diary is that of "language learning histories" which describes past events of months or years ago. Another form of a learner diary is the "difficulties diary" suggested by Tudor (1996). Students record only the problems they have experienced in the use of the language over a given period of time. Thus, the teacher can respond to whatever difficulties students face and suggest ways to help them overcome such problems. It is this particular aspect of teachers' understanding and response to the problems of language learning that we are interested in.

The purpose of this study was to sensitise teachers to the specific needs of two groups of learners studying at the Centre for English Language Communication. These are ESL undergraduates and EFL graduate students. With more foreign students, for whom English is a foreign language, enrolling at the National University of Singapore, we are faced with a greater challenge of understanding their "linguistic, social and cultural backgrounds" (Wong, 1997: 5). Therefore, we hope that by comparing the reflections of ESL and EFL learners, we would gain a better understanding of the foreign students' learning process so as to help them write and speak English effectively.

RESEARCH METHODOLOGY

Keeping a Diary

The conventional way of keeping a diary is to use a book. However, with the increasing trend towards the use of computers in language learning and teaching, the email is another means whereby students can record their reflections.

In our project, we chose email because of its rising popularity over the conventional written form of communication and its advantage of immediacy as we saw our students only twice a week and needed to respond to them quickly. Besides, the students themselves had busy schedules and were unable to meet us. This also explains why we were interested in the "difficulties diary" in a "non-introspective" way.

Collecting the Diary

Allwright and Bailey (1991) suggest that frequent periodic reviews may not be helpful as it is likely to put pressure on the students. Alternatively, they suggest a weekly discussion session where students can share some thoughts written in their diary. In addition, it is also possible to collect diaries at the end of the entire course.

With these recommendations in mind, we asked our students to keep a journal via email. Drawing from their reflections through email, we compared the difficulties in language learning, motivational level and learning strategies, of Singaporean undergraduates and Chinese postgraduates. For our study we asked the students to email us once a week from Week 2 to Week 10 of their 12-week course.

Participants

The students involved in this project were 13 first-year undergraduates from the Arts and Social Sciences Faculty and 12 postgraduate students from the Engineering Faculty. The undergraduates are all Singaporeans while the postgraduates are all from the People's Republic of China (PRC).

Profile of Singapore and PRC Students

In multiracial Singapore, English is one of the four official languages, used extensively at work, socially and professionally. Its importance as an international language and a lingua franca is well acknowledged by all Singaporeans. English is therefore used in schools as a medium of instruction for all subjects taught except the mother tongue, the language of the ethnic group to which students belong. For most Singaporean students, their mother tongue would be their first language and English, their second language. This is quite unlike the situation with the students from the PRC; in their country, Chinese is the official language and the medium of instruction in schools and universities. For the PRC students, therefore, English is taught in an EFL situation.

Students in Singapore normally spend six years in primary school, four years in secondary schools and two years in junior college. They take two major external examinations, the GCE 'O' and 'A' levels, for their English Language. Students are tested on comprehension, summary and essay writing in these two major exams. There is an oral component in the GCE 'O' level but not in the 'A' level. There are no multiple-choice questions. Similarly, an average postgraduate student from China has learned English for about 10–12 years, however, the testing is different. There are more multiple-choice questions and less written work. Moreover, there is no oral examination.

Overall, Singapore students have had 12 years of exposure to English in school. In addition, they have also been exposed to the various American and British programmes in the cinemas, and on television and radio. Furthermore, they would have had opportunities to communicate with various members of the community, local and international. Unlike the Singapore undergraduates, the postgraduates from China have not had a similar kind of exposure to English and its different varieties. Compared to their Singapore counterparts, they have fewer opportunities for using English within the community and limited exposure to English language programmes in the media.

Proficiency Course for Undergraduates and Postgraduates

At the National University of Singapore (NUS), all first-year undergraduates from the various faculties who scored a B4 and below for General Paper in the GCE 'A' level examination must take the Qualifying English Test (QET). QET is a written test set by the Centre for English Language Communication (CELC) to determine if these students need to take the English proficiency classes. They do not take an oral interview.

All postgraduate students who are foreigners and from non-English medium universities must take the Diagnostic English Test (DET), a written test set by CELC. These students also have to undergo an oral interview.

In the proficiency classes for the Arts and Social Sciences, the main objective of the course is to make the students effective readers and writers so that they can cope with their academic work. They are taught to read academic texts and to synthesise relevant ideas to complete a given task. They are also taught how to plan and write essays. They have to sit for a written examination at the end of the course.

Activities carried out in the proficiency classes for the Arts and Social Sciences Faculty and the Engineering Faculty include group discussions, peer work, and conferencing between the tutor and student. However, while undergraduates have informal oral presentations, postgraduate students have formal oral presentations. For both groups of students, the proficiency course is not an intensive one as it extends over 12 weeks with the students spending four hours each week in class, two hours per lesson.

Procedure

In the second week of the course, all students involved in the project were asked to reflect on their language learning experience. To help them focus, we gave students instructions on how to write about their reactions to class lessons, their suggestions to improve them, the difficulties they faced in learning any of the language skills, the strategies used to learn a language skill, their progress in any aspect of learning and, their feelings regarding the learning of English. They were asked to email their tutors at least once every week for a period of eight weeks regarding their learning experience. The tutors, in turn, would respond to them accordingly.

We also gave the students information on the different types of learning strategies based on the strategies mentioned by Oxford (1990) and

Chamot (1987). Chamot defines learning strategies as "techniques, or deliberate actions that students take in order to facilitate the learning and recall of both linguistic and content area information" (Chamot, 1987: 71). They were asked to indicate if they practised any of the strategies.

This study sets out to examine three main aspects: difficulties in language learning, the motivational level and learning strategies of the two groups of students.

RESULTS AND DISCUSSION

Difficulties

From the email responses, the Singaporean Arts undergraduates' difficulties were grammar, sentence structure, expression of ideas and writing skills. They reported having problems with aspects of grammar such as subject-verb agreement, tense usage and sentence construction, as illustrated in the following reflections.

"Don't realise I have so many problems with grammar."

"Writing long or very long sentences and making errors in tenses as a result; careless at times."

Other problems such as expressions and aspects of writing skills like use of connectives, organisation and development are reflected below.

"Organisation – topic sentence; long-winded."

"Sentence structure, run-on sentences and connectives. We need few connectives when writing Chinese essays." (This student took Chinese as a first language in secondary school.)

"Constructing good sentences; can't express myself well; ideas are very limited; can't develop the paragraph. Can express myself best in Chinese and find appropriate words to describe the feeling." (This student took Chinese as a first language in secondary school.)

As for the Chinese Engineering postgraduates, their difficulties are more diverse. Like the Singaporean Arts undergraduates in our study, they have problems with sentence structure, expression of ideas and writing skills, but have less difficulty with grammar generally. The following reflections reveal their difficulties.

> "One problem I met is that I often can't find the appropriate word to express my thought."

> "I feel more difficult in my writing...In my second composition writing, I repeat many words many times. The structure of composition is clear now. But the content is not clear."

> "The most difficult thing for me is how to express myself clearly, sometimes I cannot remember the words I have learned, and also I don't know how the words should be used."

> "When writing I check the exact meaning of some words and expressions and try to use them correctly. But sometimes it is hard to distinguish which should be used as a formal expression."

As can be seen, Chinese postgraduates have difficulty with expression because of limited exposure to the English language, inadequate vocabulary and the inability to use words accurately and appropriately. Like the Singaporean students, Chinese postgraduates also have difficulty with writing skills, as reflected in the following comments:

> "I hope to improve my writing ability as soon as possible. But I didn't often know how to do."

> "I've made progress in both speaking and writing, though I feel there is still difficulty for me to write a paper."

These students also reported problems with speaking and listening skills.

> "The big problem is oral English and listening."

> "Another problem is my listening which I think is the poorest part. If people speak clearly and not so fast, I can understand, but if they speak fast and connect words together or use unfamiliar expressions, I can't understand."

"I have told you that my listening comprehension is not very good. I think the reason is my pronunciation, at some time I don't understand the words from their pronunciation, even I know their spell very well."

"My problem in English studying is little confidence to speak out."

From the above reflections, the Chinese postgraduates' problems in oral/aural skills range from limited vocabulary, pace and connected speech of interlocutors, to poor pronunciation due to lack of confidence. A further problem they face is the limited opportunities for practising speaking and listening on campus because of the large population of Singaporean Chinese and Chinese nationals in NUS. As a result, they often converse in Chinese. Hence, a postgraduate commented:

"...there are so many persons around us who can speak Chinese. The result is the reduce force to improve English."

Both groups of students have learnt English for more than ten years, but their language proficiency level is inadequate to meet the requirements of academic and professional work. The apparent reasons for the unsatisfactory command of English for the two groups differ vastly. One possible reason is that for the Singaporean undergraduates, the emphasis on group work under the communicative approach has led to reduced instruction and practice in grammar and structure (Khoo, 1995). In addition, from the educationists' point of view, there has been a decline in the use of standard spoken English due to the popular use of Singlish and code-mixing. Indeed, to counteract this decline in standard spoken English, the government launched a Speak Good English Movement in April 2000. Added to this, a number of teachers have complained that students are not reading enough outside of class. On the other hand, from the numerous complaints we read in the papers and from our own experience, having taught in schools for several years, the heavy workload of English teachers in both primary and secondary schools (large classes of about 40, and innumerable written assignments and extra duties) leave them with little time and energy to give personal attention to individual students' language needs. Consequently, these undergraduates are generally fluent, but they are only fairly accurate in their utterances, and this affects the way they write. Hence, their writing lacks grammatical accuracy, syntactical maturity and precision of expression even after 12 years of English language instruction.

For the Chinese postgraduates, English has been learned as a foreign language and hence, they have had few opportunities to practise speaking and listening skills; besides, their oral English has never been tested and assessed. This is why they have difficulties in oral communication, especially in the initial period after their arrival in Singapore. In particular, students have expressed to their teachers that they have difficulties understanding the English of Singaporeans, Indian nationals and other nationalities, having been exposed only to American English (Voice of America programmes being very popular in China). Secondly, because of the differences in structure and word usage between Chinese and English, these students when using translation to facilitate communication make mistakes in word choice and expressions. And as their language learning experience in China required them to write a short guided essay, students have had little practice and awareness about organisation and development of ideas, aspects of coherence and cohesion, tone and style in their writing.

Between the two groups, from what we have learned about their language background, the Chinese postgraduates had more difficulties with the language than the Singaporean undergraduates, and consequently, their anxiety levels were higher, as revealed in their reflections.

> "Sometimes I'm afraid to talk to someone in English language. My brain empty. I'm too nervous to answer it."

> "My project needs me to work in the refining plant from March 1st. I was told that the guys in that plant will talk with me fastly by English. I was a little nervous about this, my listening English is not very good, but this project will be decided by my performance, I must get the customers' trust at the beginning time. Can you give me any advices on enhancing my listening in two weeks?"

Most Chinese postgraduates have hinted that they face a lot of pressure in their communication with their supervisors because of the need to convey ideas on their research in English, and the need to understand their supervisors' instructions given in English. The many kinds of English accents of teaching staff in NUS can pose listening difficulties for Chinese postgraduates and it is possible that many of these Chinese students may be too embarrassed or shy to ask their supervisors to repeat their instructions. Communicating well with their supervisors is particularly important as they are expected to carry out research independently unlike in China where they were given close supervision. They also have to attend classes that are conducted in English, and do assignments that require them to write as many as 3,000 words compared to the 150-word assignments at the College English Examinations. In addition, they have to make seminar presentations in English and respond to questions in English. They also need to complete a 40,000-word dissertation in order to fulfil the Masters' requirements, a task that seems daunting as they have never written a research report in English before coming to study in NUS.

The heavy course and research load and the different style of supervision coupled with the lack of an adequate proficiency in the language have led to anxiety for Chinese postgraduate students. Hilleson (1996) similarly noted the high anxiety of foreign scholars in an English-medium school in Singapore. Campbell and Ortiz (cited in Hilleson, 1996: 273) also observed "alarming levels of anxiety in post-secondary students enrolled in foreign language courses in competitive environments". Thus it is likely that the above comments such as "nervous" and "this project will be decided by my performance" indicate some degree of anxiety and the stress for the foreign students trying to perfect their English.

Motivation

It is therefore not surprising that the Chinese postgraduates are more motivated in their language learning than the Singaporean Arts undergraduates. The reflections of the Chinese students show that they desire to be more proficient in English so that they can perform well in their studies and to achieve a successful career. Some examples of these are presented in the following statements:

"English is the main language in Singapore. Not only in daily life but also in my research work, English plays a more and more important role in my life. So I have to pay much attention to it."

"The big problem is oral English and listening. Please give some suggestion so that I am able to make a great progress with my English."

"I think if I have enough time, I will study hard on English language. Because I know it is so important for me to do everything in the future."

"I understand how to prepare for a presentation, how to...They are important in my future job."

Thus, for the Chinese students, English language learning is viewed as important for academic and professional success. It is significant that there was no evidence of similar motivation for language learning in the reflections of the Singapore students. They perceive their command of the language to be adequate since they are able to use the language for social and academic purposes and have managed to pass major exams as well as their English Proficiency courses.

We observe that the motivation to learn the language also increased with perceived success among the weaker students of both groups, as seen in the following reports of students of lower proficiency. Reflections from the Chinese postgraduate students and Singaporean undergraduates respectively are reproduced below.

"My proficiency level of English language has gotten some progress, especially in effective communication, writing and oral ability. Now I have enough courage to talk to others in the English language. I am not afraid of writing, have found some effective ways to improve the weakest sides from the course and by you. As time pass, I will make a big jump in my English language."

"Through your feedback, I knew that I make fewer grammar errors now and I am happy that I do make some progress. I know that I am still far from B+ and I will work harder."

One could sense the motivation to work hard at raising proficiency in these reflections of the weaker students from both groups who had been given the needed support and guidance. However, for the more proficient Singaporean undergraduates in the course, motivation was low, as they did not think they had made vast improvements in the many years of language learning. The "plateau" effect of progress in language learning had set in. Besides, they believed that their ability to communicate fluently though not accurately is adequate for functioning in academic and professional situations. Therefore they tend to be complacent, as seen in their low frequency of email responses and minimal efforts in their course assignments.

Another reason for this "relaxed" attitude towards the English course, also evident among some Chinese postgraduates, is that the English proficiency course is viewed as a subsidiary subject and regarded as less important than their content-based courses, and when the pressure is on, it receives little attention. They feel that they have "more important" tasks such as course work, research and writing assignments to attend to. However, for the Chinese postgraduates, motivation continued to be high as they believe that being able to communicate accurately and fluently is the prerequisite for achieving academic and professional success. Besides, the demands of their Masters' degree course did not seem to allow them sufficient time for learning English. This internal conflict is expressed in the following reflections of the Chinese postgraduates, something not evident among those of the Singaporean undergraduates.

> "Although I am clear that my English is poor and I need to enhance my abilities on writing, speaking, listening of English, at present I have to work hard on reading and writing papers."

> " I think the most efficient way is that during one period of time studying English is the task to face. In fact, it will save time. But now when leaving English class we have to do something more important. Then the time left for English learning is too little."

As we can see, in general, the two groups differ considerably in their motivation towards learning English, due to differences in proficiency levels and attitudes about language learning.

Strategies

We noticed that the students' email responses focused on the skills they have problems with, and their strategy use was limited mainly to direct strategies and socio-affective factors. Results from a questionnaire containing a comprehensive list of strategies compiled by Chamot showed a wider range of strategies. In our analysis of strategies, we will focus on the important strategies common to both groups, as the differences seem minor.

Both groups reported seeking help from the tutor and working together with tutorial mates as important strategies they use in language learning.

> "Sorry I have another composition for you. Please have a look at it. There are many things to be improved. I hope I can get the improvements from you."

> "I think I should do more practice to improve my English skill. Could you please give us some advises? With your help, we can improve our English skill quickly."

> "Learned a lot from others' achievement."

> "Find out what's wrong in my own speaking from others' speaking."

> "I learned a lot from your comments and the feedback of others."

> "I like discussion that let me not afraid to speak in English even though I will do something wrong."

> "Reading peers' essays; asking teacher to help in writing skills."

> "Have peer and conferencing activities to help each other and spot errors."

> "Ask tutor for help."

Young's (1987) study of Chinese children indicated that they were more adult-oriented learners than non-Chinese children, and therefore looked more consistently to their teachers for guidance and support than they did to one another. Our postgraduates' email responses seem to suggest that this is not true for Chinese postgraduates. As they are older, they are willing to learn from both tutor and peers.

Also, the email responses of the postgraduates in our study do not support Melton's (1990) findings on "Chinese Students' Learning Style Preferences". Unlike the Chinese postgraduates in our study, her Chinese students (in China) did not like group learning. The responses we have received from the students are consistent with those of Chu et al.'s (1997) study, which revealed that both Chinese postgraduates in NUS and Singaporean students like group learning. The difference between our findings and Melton's may be due to the fact that the Chinese students in our study, who had never had the experience of group work in China, have been exposed to it here and have developed a liking for it.

Other strategies both groups employed were reading and practising in the respective skills of focus. The Singaporean undergraduates did writing and grammar exercises, while the Chinese postgraduates were engaged in listening, speaking and writing activities. Both groups also read recommended reference books. For example, the Singaporean undergraduates consulted grammar reference books; the Chinese postgraduates read books on writing. Both groups also liked to learn to write by examining writing models. The following extracts from their reflections in Table 1 illustrate the popular use of these strategies.

Table 1. Popular Strategies used by both Chinese Postgraduates and Singaporean Undergraduates

Read on different subjects
Read CNN text
Watch films
Talk to English-speaking colleagues
Read my peers' essays
Read newspapers
Listen to BBC
Write emails
Practice speaking
Learn from example you gave

We noted that our students were actively using some of the above-mentioned strategies, and yet were asking for more ways to improve their proficiency, as seen in the following reflections:

> "I think I should do more practice to improve my English skill. Could you please give us some advises? With your help, we can improve our English skill quickly."

> "I want to make use of my every spare time to learn English. Can you please give me some advice on how to improve my English step by step?"

From our conversations with individual students who expressed frustration and impatience over the seemingly slow returns for their efforts, we realise that our students follow their teachers' advice without assessing their particular needs, and hence, they are not clear about the purpose for adopting a piece of given advice. Vann and Abraham (1990) noted in their study that unsuccessful learners were active strategy users, but they applied strategies inappropriately. They suggested that unsuccessful learners lacked higher-order processes or metacognitive strategies, which would enable them to use the relevant strategies to meet their linguistic needs. In our study, we observed this to be true, as both groups rarely reported using metacognitive strategies such as analysing linguistic demands, reflecting on language learning and self-monitoring. Hence, most of our students chose inappropriate strategies.

For example, a student listened to BBC news regularly, thinking somehow it would improve his English. But when asked why he was listening to BBC news, he said it would help to raise his proficiency. But at the same time, he complained he was unable to follow most of it. When the teacher probed further to find out why he had difficulty following the BBC news, she discovered the reason to be his poor pronunciation. The teacher then helped the student to arrive at his objective for listening: to improve his pronunciation. She directed him to obtain the text, listen to how it was read, and examine whether there were differences between his pronunciation and the newsreader's. And this gradually enabled him to listen with better understanding.

Similarly, our students often told us that they were reading the newspapers to improve their English, but saw no improvement in their proficiency. After making our students analyse their problems, we directed them to the appropriate sections of the newspaper, such as the *Forum Page* in *The Straits Times* on social issues, or the lighter sections of the paper, where articles of general interest are located. They were encouraged to read these, and collect vocabulary of specified categories for learning, review and use. Consequently, they commented that reading such sections had exposed them to words of general use which, in turn, had increased their grasp of word meanings and their use.

From the above reflections and our observations, it is obvious that both groups of students need help in identifying their specific needs, guidance in choosing effective strategies and setting clear goals for themselves so that they can measure their achievements. Giving them broad unfocused traditional advice such as "read more, listen more" is like throwing them prematurely into the deep ocean.

As we were concerned about the difficulties with expression by both groups, we specially noted the use of strategies related to vocabulary learning. We found that *contextualisation*, that is, placing a word/phrase in a meaningful context which aids the accurate use of a word/phrase, and *grouping* which helps systematic, efficient learning and retention of vocabulary, were among the less popularly used strategies for the two groups. In fact, the Chinese group reported fewer instances of these strategies. This finding is consistent with those of Chamot, Kupper and Impink-Hernandez (cited in O'Malley and Chamot, 1990: 123). These strategies were among the lower frequency strategies cited by high school ESL students and native English-speaking students learning a foreign language. The infrequent use of *grouping* and *contextualisation* may partly account for the problem with expression of ideas by both groups, the problem being more acute for the Chinese postgraduate students. So, in terms of the repertoire of strategies, both groups do not differ significantly. They need to increase their use of metacognitive strategies and vocabulary-related cognitive strategies.

CONCLUSION

We set out to do a diary study of students' reflections over a period of eight weeks, but due to the tight schedule of our students and the fact that their English course was not intensive, comprising a total of four hours weekly, the students on average emailed us only two–three times. Reflections were brief and focused on difficulties they faced. Hence, our study in reality was a "difficulties" e-diary, reflecting and seeking help at the same time.

Our study, which compared Singaporean undergraduates with Chinese postgraduates in terms of their difficulties, motivation and learning strategies, shows that the Chinese group had more difficulties, but were more motivated learners than the Singaporean group. In terms of strategy use, they were similar. Both groups needed to choose more effective strategies for efficient learning of the language.

IMPLICATIONS FROM OUR STUDY

Several practical implications may be derived from our study:

- The learning philosophy of intermediate ESL learners has to be broadened so that they would realise that language learning requires attention to both function and form in order to be able to function adequately in both academic and professional settings. To offset stagnation in language learning, Harmer (1998) suggests that they should be shown what they still need to learn, be assigned challenging tasks and made to analyse language more thoroughly.
- The multifaceted language difficulties faced by the EFL postgraduates in a new challenging academic environment has led to high anxiety, which could be debilitating or facilitating. Tutors must be sensitive to this, and seek to create a conducive learning environment to reduce stress and promote learning.
- Both Singapore undergraduates and Chinese postgraduates need guidance in identifying needs, choice of relevant strategies and setting of realistic goals. To increase vocabulary mastery, they need to be given practice in the strategies of contextualisation and grouping.
- Classroom instruction of writing skills, grammar and structure in the secondary schools needs to be re-examined to strengthen Singapore students' accurate use of the language and written skills.
- ESL/EFL students should be encouraged to write "difficulties" diaries as part of their learning programme. Whether in email form or on loose-leaf sheets of paper, they serve as a channel of

communication with the teacher, providing a means of getting specific help and feedback for effective teaching and learning. In addition, they serve to reduce anxiety level, especially for the EFL learner and, they can become an avenue for reflection on learning and provide encouragement to work independently on specific skills or strategies.

However, our study has one major limitation in the quantitative aspect. For practical reasons already outlined in the opening section of this article, our study was based on a small group of Singaporean undergraduates and Chinese postgraduates. The results of this study cannot be generalised for the population of all Singaporean undergraduates or Chinese postgraduates. A follow-up study involving bigger pools of students would be needed for empirical testing and validations of the observations made in this exploratory study.

REFERENCES

Allwright, D. & Bailey, K. M. (1991). *Focus on the Language Classroom: An Introduction to Classroom Research for Language Teachers.* Cambridge: Cambridge University Press.

Bailey, K. M. (1991). Diary studies of classroom language learning: The doubting game and the believing game. In E. Sadtono (Ed.), *Language Acquisition and the Second/Foreign Language Classroom* (pp. 60–102). SEAMEO Anthology Series no. 28. Singapore: SEAMEO Regional Language Centre.

Bailey, K. M. & Ochsner, R. (1983). A methodological review of the diary studies: Windmill tilting or social science? In K. M. Bailey, M. Long & S. Peck (Eds.), *Second Language Acquisition Studies* (pp. 188–98). Rowley, Mass: Newbury House.

Chamot, A. U. (1987). The learning strategies of ESL. In A. Wenden & J. Rubin (Eds.), *Learning Strategies in Language Learning* (pp. 71–83). Englewood Cliffs, NJ: Prentice Hall.

Chu, L.; Kitchen, T. & Chew, M. L. (1997). How do we learn best?: Preferences and strategies in learning and teaching styles at the National University of Singapore. *STETS Language and Communication Review,* 1997(1): 14–32.

Harmer, J. (1998). *How to Teach English.* Essex: Addison Wesley Longman Limited.

Hilleson, M. (1996). I want to talk with them, but I don't want them to hear: An introspective study of second language anxiety in an English-medium school. In K. M. Bailey & D. Nunan (Eds.), *Voices from the Language Classroom* (pp. 248–75). New York: Cambridge University Press.

Khoo, R. (1995). Communicative language teaching and the 'Singapore English' classroom — An assessment. In Teng and Ho (Eds.), *The English Language in Singapore: Implications for Teaching* (pp. 19–28). Singapore: Singapore Association for Applied Linguistics.

Matsumoto, K. (1989). An analysis of a Japanese ESL learner's diary: Factors involved in the L2 learning process. *JALT Journal*, 11(2): 167–92.

_____ (1996). Helping L2 learners reflect on classroom learning. *ELT Journal*, 50(2): 143–49.

Melton, C. (1990). Bridging the cultural gap: A study of Chinese students' learning style preferences. *RELC Journal*, 21(1): 29–54.

O'Malley, J. M. & Chamot, A. U. (1990). *Learning Strategies in Second Language Acquisition*. Cambridge: Cambridge University Press.

Oxford, R. L. (1990). *Language Learning Strategies: What Every Teacher Should Know*. New York: Newsbury House Publishers.

Oxford, R. L. & Green, J. M. (1996). Language learning histories: Learners and teachers helping each other understand learning styles and strategies. *TESOL Journal*, 6(1): 20–23.

Tudor, I. (1996). *Learner-centredness as Language Education*. Cambridge: Cambridge University Press.

Vann, R. J. & Abraham, R. G. (1990). Strategies of unsuccessful language learners. *TESOL Quarterly*, 24: 177–98.

Wenden, A. L. (1991). *Learner Strategies for Learner Autonomy*. London: Prentice Hall.

Wenden, A. L. & Rubin, J. (1987). *Learner Strategies in Language Learning*. London: Prentice Hall.

Wong, L. A. (1997). The teaching of English and Communication Skills in Singapore tertiary institutions: Current situation and future directions. *STETS Language and Communication Review*, 1997(1): 3–6.

Young, R. (1987). The cultural context of TESOL — A review of research into Chinese classrooms. *RELC Journal*, 18(2): 15–30.

CHAPTER 5

PRC Students and Group Work — Their Actions and Reactions

J.E. LISA MEYER

INTRODUCTION

The use of group work tasks (GWTs)[1] in language and communication classes is supported by learning theory, writing theory, workplace reality, and studies showing positive student attitudes. Since the bulk of this research is Euro-North American based, many of our guidelines and expectations for GWTs and small group negotiation are highly influenced by Western cultural norms. However, the effectiveness of group work in any particular setting depends on affective factors including students' attitudes towards doing group work and students' behaviour while doing the group work. Teachers must have an understanding of these affective factors and their influences when they make their decisions regarding the administration and evaluation of classroom GWTs. Whether a learning activity is beneficial depends to a great extent on whether the students deem it to be a useful methodology (Brown, 1994). It is also important that a teacher's expectation of student behaviour matches what the students are willing to do or are comfortable with doing. For example, Carson and Nelson (1994) point out that writing groups from collectivist cultures such as the People's Republic of China (PRC) may not behave the same way as Western writing groups would. We would then need to question the effectiveness of such common GWT techniques as peer review in PRC and other Asian settings (Garratt, 1995).

---

[1]In this paper, I define a GWT to be any classroom task which requires students to write in groups. This would normally be a one-product-one-group task.

Apart from studies by Carson and Nelson (1994, 1996) and Cortazzi and Jin (1996), there is very little record of the attitudes toward, or behaviour during GWTs of students from PRC. This lack of information for PRC students is problematic for many of us teaching at the Centre for English Language Communication (CELC) at the National University of Singapore (NUS). CELC teaches English for academic and business purposes to undergraduate and graduate-level students from the People's Republic of China (PRC). Many of us use GWTs with our PRC students, but do so without the awareness of how our students feel about the tasks, and how they behave while working on such tasks.

Thus, the purpose of my research was to gauge the attitude and behaviour of two groups of students from PRC regarding GWTs in the language classroom. Specifically, my questions were:

- Do the students prefer group work or individual work?
- Do the students seem to be more group oriented or more individualistic?
- Which behaviour is more predominant — being forthright or maintaining group harmony?
- How do the students measure their own success in a group project?
- How do the students feel about peer feedback?
- How reliant are the students on their teacher?

The results were to help teachers decide whether or not to continue with GWTs, and, if so, make any necessary modifications to the way in which we administer and evaluate GWTs.

In this chapter I first offer a review of the literature regarding the use of group writing in the classroom, and culturally influenced differences in behaviour in GWTs. I then outline my research methods and findings, and discuss the implications for teaching. I conclude by discussing the question of whether we should pursue GWTs with PRC students.

SUPPORT FOR GROUP WRITING TASKS

Learning Theory

According to the social constructionist view of learning and knowledge, we make meaning of new things we encounter through the social interaction necessary to become part of a new community. Knowledge is a social process (Bruffee, 1981), not a product to be passed on by a lecturer. Bakhtin (cited in Weiss, 1991) agrees, saying that understanding is dialogic and active, not passive. It can be argued, then, that learning through collaboration is superior to learning in isolation. How does new understanding come about through interaction? We learn through negotiating differences (Bakhtin, cited in Weiss, 1991) and confrontation (Morgan and Murray, 1991). And confrontation, and responding to confrontation, naturally are more likely to occur during collaboration than in individual work.

It may also be that a student will learn better in a setting where the asymmetrical distribution of power and monopoly of expertise found in a traditional teacher-centred classroom have been replaced by a more egalitarian atmosphere (Trimbur, 1989). This assumption has led to the common inclusion of peer reviewing and peer assessment in GWTs. Successful peer feedback and assessment sessions in GWTs result in the development of critical thinking skills and promote active and teacher-independent learning (Cheng and Warren, 1996). Improved learner autonomy should also occur as students learn inductively through experience together with their peers, rather than from lectures by the teacher.

Writing Theory and Better Writing

Communication is inherently collaborative and social — it is the "building of bridges between writer and reader, or listener and speaker" (Voloshinov, 1986:102). We would expect a GWT, especially one involving peer feedback, to foster such collaborative communication more than an individual writing task would.

The achievement of better writing skills, and the development of better writers through group writing tasks has been documented in the research literature. Johnson and Johnson (1993) found that cooperative learning led to higher individual achievement in writing than did individual learning. Tebeaux (1991) found that students' sensitivity to audience and tone was enhanced through cooperative writing. Van Pelt and Gillam (1991) describe a case where a student involved in a GWT moved from being an insecure writer who looked to the teacher for all judgements to a more confident writer who looked to herself and her peers for judgement and constructive criticism.

Workplace Writing

If our goal is to prepare our students for the workplace, in a Business English course for example, we need to expose students to writing situations and processes similar to those they will find themselves in the workplace. One of the features of the information society we now live in is that collaboration is replacing the competitive and individualistic ethos existing in the Euro-North American industrial society to date (Trimbur, 1989). This manifests itself in the common occurrence of collaborative writing in the workplace (Anderson, 1985; Casari and Povlacs, 1988; Faigley and Miller, 1982; Killingsworth and Jones, 1989; Van Pelt and Gillam, 1991). We can therefore conclude that GWTs will more nearly approximate workplace experience than classroom tasks done individually.

Attitude toward GWTs

North American studies have reported generally positive student attitudes toward GWTs and peer review done in tertiary level courses (Battalio, 1993; Duin, Jorn and DeBower, 1991; Scott, 1988; Shirk, 1991; Wickliffe,1997). However, among the Asia-based studies involving Chinese students, there seem to be no conclusive findings regarding attitude toward group versus individual work. Chu, Chew and Kitchen (1997) and Stebbins (1995) found no clear preference for either mode of learning, although Flowerdew (1998), Meyer (1999) and Roskams (1999) did find a preference for group work. There have also been mixed findings regarding student attitude toward peer review, feedback and evaluation in writing tasks. Attitude toward peer review has been found to be both positive (Garratt, 1995; Roskams, 1999) and negative (Mangelsdorf, 1992). Attitude toward peer evaluation has been found to be mixed (Cheng and Warren, 1996) to positive (Conway, Kember, Sivan and Wu, 1993).

There is a greater consensus among researchers that Chinese students have a feeling of collectivism and that therefore group work would seem to be an appropriate mode of learning for Chinese students (Cortazzi and Jin, 1996; Meyer, 1999; Nelson, 1995; Roskams, 1999). Within the Confucian tradition, students learn through co-operation, by working for the common good, by supporting each other and by not elevating themselves above others (Nelson, 1995: 9).

> ...in Chinese society — and in the classroom — the priorities are that each person must be part of a group or community; learning interdependency, co-operation and social awareness...Collective consciousness [has been] a significant aspect of Chinese traditional values since Confucius and a strong element in Chinese approaches to learning.
>
> (Cortazzi and Jin, 1996, p.178)

However, Cortazzi and Jin (1996) point out that Chinese students tend to work collaboratively outside the classroom, but in the classroom expect the teacher to give knowledge, since traditionally, Asian students expect the teacher to take charge and act as the provider of information, and source of learning. This has been confirmed in the studies by Meyer (1999) and Zhang (1995), who found that students showed a preference for teacher feedback over peer feedback. Roskams (1999), however, found that students in Hong Kong were fairly neutral as to whether they preferred teacher or peer feedback on their writing.

Cultural Differences in Group Work

The less conclusive Asian findings regarding student attitude and behaviour regarding classroom group work may be explained by cultural differences. The differences in belief and behaviour relevant to group work between the Euro-North American culture and other cultures have been discussed by Bosley (1993), Carson and Nelson (1994) and Gudykunst and Hammer (1983). The key differences they have described are as follows.

- Euro-North Americans value the individual above the group. Many other cultures value the group above the individual. "In 70% of cultures throughout the world, the needs of the family, community, and even corporations come before those of any one person" (Bosley, 1993:117).
- In many non-Western cultures achievement is measured in terms of how many contributions an individual makes to his or her group's general welfare. An individual is successful if he or she

preserves his or her position in a social structure. Success is not measured in terms of how well the individual distinguishes himself or herself from the rest of the group. Regarding group writing in particular, Carson and Nelson (1994) say that writing groups from collectivist cultures such as the PRC function for the benefit of the group rather than the individual and that group members are more concerned with group harmony than individual contribution. This means that the individual assessment crucial for successful group work by Bosley (1993) may not be appropriate for people from these other cultures. If individual responsibility is emphasised, that person's relationships within his or her group may be undermined. Generally "students from cultures that believe in group harmony and balance may not live up to Euro-North American expectations of appropriate group behaviour" (Bosley, 1993:56).

- Euro-North American culture highly regards individuals who can make their own decisions. However, in the Middle East and Asia, it is considered rude and shameful to make a decision on one's own; to do so is to ignore the importance of collective decisions (Bosley, 1993:55). This means Asian students will make statements they feel are best for the group's harmony, even if that's not what they personally believe. Self-disclosure may be a behaviour alien to them, according to Gudykunst and Hammer (1983). This could mean that activities such as peer review might not be as effective for non-Western students. As both Carson and Nelson (1994) and Garratt (1995) point out, active participation in peer reviewing and giving meaningful feedback may be problematic for Asians due to the Asian's fear of making mistakes and thus losing face, and the Asian politeness norm which prioritises group harmony.

- Conflict and dissensus, rather than consensus, in group work are now encouraged in Euro-North American classrooms, but this is not the norm in many classrooms in other cultures. Gudykunst and Hammer (1983) state that confrontation is behaviour limited primarily to white, middle-class people.

However, we do not know whether these descriptions are in fact reflected in the reality of any given context involving Asian students. Meyer (1999) found that undergraduate students in Singapore are actually quite "Western" in their behaviour during GWTs. Although they fit the Asian stereotype of being group-oriented and teacher-dependent, they do not necessarily put group harmony before confronting conflict. They feel that open confrontation is acceptable behaviour in group work, and are fairly forthright in stating their opinions, even if these opinions oppose others' in the group. In addition, these students feel contributions by an individual to the end product are a more important measurement of success than contributing to group harmony.

RESEARCH SETTING AND METHODOLOGY

The subjects of my research were two groups of PRC students studying at the NUS. Group One consisted of students doing a pre-university six-month intensive English Proficiency (EP) and English for Academic Purposes (EAP) course. They did this course immediately after arriving in Singapore. These were students who had been in their first year at Chinese universities and were, on average, at an intermediate level of English proficiency. Their average age was 18 and about 70% were male.

Group Two consisted of PRC graduate students doing a 10-week Business English course, a required module for the MBA programme they were doing at the NUS. The medium of instruction in all their other MBA modules was Chinese. Most of the students had either just arrived in Singapore from PRC or had been in Singapore for only one or two years. Their average age was 30, and about 70% were male.

Both groups completed a questionnaire asking about their attitude toward and their behaviour during classroom group work. (See Appendix A.) For Group One, all the students from five randomly selected classes (N=100) completed the questionnaire toward the end of their six-month course. They had just completed a fairly extensive group project involving an oral presentation and a written report. Two of the teachers of the five classes were North American, and three were Chinese, from Singapore and Hong Kong. For Group Two, all the students from four randomly selected classes (N=65) completed the questionnaire toward the end of their Business English course. The students had worked in groups on both written and oral projects throughout the course. Three of the teachers were North American, and one was Singaporean Chinese.

FINDINGS AND IMPLICATIONS FOR TEACHING

I have used the findings of the questionnaire to answer my six major research questions below. The numbers in parenthesis following each question refer to the question numbers of the questionnaire.

Research Question 1: Do the students prefer group work or individual work? (1)

Since 81% of the Group Two learners prefer group work as a mode of learning (see Table 1), it appears that for graduate-level PRC students, group work tasks will at least meet a positive reception. However, for about 50% of the Group One learners, teachers may have to make some effort to "sell" group work tasks, and to ensure a more enjoyable experience. For these younger students, group membership needs to be carefully considered — perhaps agreed upon jointly by students and teacher, and the time spent by the group on the assigned tasks needs to be carefully monitored. If the younger students have not had much experience with group work, they have trouble meeting some of the common challenges of group work such as team building, team management and task management. I would suggest going over these aspects of group work with the students, and sharing with them the tips for success in these areas provided by the students in Meyer's (1999) paper.

Table 1. Results of Question #1: Learning Style Preference (%)

Response	Group one	Group two
Group work	53	81
Individual work	47	19

Research Question 2: Do the students seem to be more group oriented or more individualistic? (2–4)

From the results in Table 2, I would conclude that there is no clear indication that the Group One students are either group-oriented or

Table 2. Results of Questions #2–4: Attitudes Toward Co-operation (%)

Question #	Group	Response		
		Group	Individual	Hard to say
2. Which do you value more	1	23	27	50
highly?	2	54	14	32
3. Do you learn through		Yes	No	Can't say
co-operation?	1	41	23	35
	2	55	20	25
4. Do you feel you need to be		Yes	No	
part of a group?	1	55	45	
	2	72	28	

individualistic. This would probably explain why only a small majority of them found group work more enjoyable than individual work. I might speculate that their tendency to be rather more individualistic than we would expect arises in part from the competitive nature of the education system in China.

The graduate students, on the other hand, are fairly clearly group-oriented, more in line with our Asian stereotype. I would speculate that this orientation comes from their workplace experiences. Most may, however, not be consciously aware of what they can gain through co-operative learning. Indeed, 35% of the graduate students could not say whether they learn through co-operation at all. Therefore, it may be advisable to introduce to both groups of students the benefits of co-operative learning (Bruffee, 1973; Johnson and Johnson, 1993; Roskams, 1999). A conscious awareness of the benefits may act to convince some of the more sceptical and individualistic students. For any sceptical graduate-level students, it may be even more effective to share with them the advantages of collaborative writing in the workplace, which include gaining from multiple perspectives on the topic and format, relieving the tedium of writing alone, and improving the quality of the final document.

Research Question 3: Which behaviour is more predominant — being forthright or maintaining group harmony? (6–13)

The clear majority in both groups of students reported that confrontation (open disagreement) quite commonly occurs during group work and that this is acceptable behaviour in group work (see Table 3). Among the older students, however, confrontation was reportedly slightly less common, and there was slightly less agreement that this is acceptable behaviour.

Supporting this finding, most students said that they would state openly if they disagree with something being discussed rather than just agree to maintain group harmony, and stated that they are forthright about making suggestions for improvement of the project work.

However, in both groups the students are not so forthright about declining to take on more work than they feel they should if asked to do so by other group members. In addition, in neither group are students so forthright about confronting a group member who is doing poor or inappropriate work. Although I am aware of no documentation of how Western group members behave in such circumstances, we might suspect similar avoidance in such delicate situations. Finally, the majority in both groups reported that they do sometimes make statements or agree with other group members just to maintain group harmony, even if what they say is not what they personally believe.

In conclusion, it seems there may be a slight tendency to act to maintain group harmony, though perhaps not to the extreme we might expect from the stereotypical description of Asian behaviour. Most of the students reported that they do not hesitate to admit they do not understand something or ask for clarification within their peer groups. The stereotypical Asian hesitancy to disclose one's own inadequacies so as not to lose face does not seem to hold true for the two groups of PRC students studied here.

Research Question 4: How do the students measure their own success in a group project? (5)

The slight tendency to value the maintenance of group harmony (seen in the discussion above of research question 5) is reflected in the fact

Table 3. Results of Questions #6–13: Confrontation-related Attitude and Behaviour (%)

Question #	Group	Response			
6. How common is confrontation?		Never	Rare	Sometimes	Common
	1	2	8	55	35
	2	0	23	48	29
7. Is confrontation in group work acceptable?		No	Yes		
	1	16	84		
	2	27	73		
8. Do you ever make a statement or agree just to maintain group harmony?		Never	Seldom	Sometimes	Often
	1	5	28	60	7
	2	4	17	68	11
9. What do you do if you don't agree with a group mate?		Definite no	Disagree tactfully	Agree, for group harmony	Agree, to finish work quickly
	1	25	63	7	5
	2	29	63	6	2
10. How do you respond if a group member asks you to do more work?		Definite no	Disagree tactfully	Agree, for group harmony	Agree, to finish work quickly
	1	15	39	18	27
	2	9	46	19	26
11. Do you admit you don't understand?		Never	Seldom	Sometimes	Often
	1	2	23	13	62
	2	3	2	26	69
12. Do you complain about a group member's work?		Yes	No, to avoid embarrassment	No, to finish work quickly	
	1	48	28	24	
	2	45	32	23	
13. Point out faults with group project?		No, to finish work quickly	No, to avoid appearing foolish	Yes	
	1	7	3	90	
	2	12	8	80	

Table 4.   Results of Question #5: Measurement of Success (%)

Group	Response				
	Contribution to group's welfare	Contribution to group harmony	Contribution to final product	Active participation	Contribution of ideas
Group One	39	34	57	35	66
Group Two	12	40	74	31	65

that 34% of the Group One students and 40% of the Group Two students stated that they measure, at least in part, their success in a group work project based on the degree to which they have helped to maintain group harmony (see Table 4). However, a larger number (60% from Group One and 70% from Group Two) stated that they measure their own success using more typically Western criteria — that is, how many good ideas they had contributed throughout the project, and how much they had actually contributed to the final product.

The findings for research questions 3 and 4 have implications in the area of group work evaluation. Many of us feel that in order to make evaluation of a group-produced product fairer to all group members, there must be some evaluation of individual contribution. Bosley (1993), however, warns us that it may not be appropriate to assess the individual contributions to a group project made by students from non-Euro-North American cultures, since they hesitate to behave individualistically, or in a way which would jeopardise group harmony. In the present study, nonetheless, the majority of my PRC students rate their own success based on their individual contributions, and for most, maintaining group harmony does not seem to be of over-riding importance. Therefore, I believe rating individual contributions, if a teacher deems this to be necessary or beneficial, would not be inappropriate for these PRC students.

Research Question 5: How do the students feel about peer feedback? (14–20)

The results of questionnaire questions 14 to 20 (see Table 5) reveal that both groups of students have positive feelings about peer feedback,

Table 5. Results of Questions #14–21: Attitudes About Peer Review (%)

Question #	Group	Response		
14. Comfortable with receiving compliments from group-mates?		Yes	No	
	1	70	29	
	2	68	32	
15. Comfortable with receiving feedback from group-mates?		No problem	A little uncomfortable	Very uncomfortable
	1	59	37	3
	2	80	18	2
16. Do you value your group-mates' feedback?		Greatly	Somewhat	Not really
	1	31	65	3
	2	66	34	0
17. Comfortable with receiving feedback from non-group-mates?		No problem	A little uncomfortable	Very uncomfortable
	1	69	27	4
	2	77	21	2
18. Do you value the feedback from non-group-mates?		Greatly	Somewhat	Not really
	1	33	65	2
	2	60	38	2
19. Comfortable with giving feedback to another group?		No problem	A little uncomfortable	Very uncomfortable
	1	60	32	8
	2	62	35	3
20. Prefer feedback from classmates or teacher?		Classmates	Teacher	No preference (equal)
	1	3	60	37
	2	5	46	49
21. Which do you expect your teacher to do more of?		Give knowledge	Guide you to gain knowledge yourself	
	1	13	85	
	2	18	82	

which seems to support the findings above regarding their lack of hesitancy to disclose their ideas for improvement of the project work and to admit a lack of understanding. This would also support the findings of Garratt (1995) and Roskams (1999) who reported positive attitudes toward peer review.

All the students studied here felt fairly comfortable with giving peer feedback. Both groups of students said they were fairly comfortable with receiving feedback from their group members, though the MBA students felt more comfortable with this. (The younger students were more comfortable with receiving feedback from peers outside of their group.) This would suggest that the younger students need to be taught the value of peer feedback, that is students can learn more in a relatively non-threatening community of peers than they can working alone (Artemeva and Logie, 2000; Lockhart and Ng, 1993; Mangelsdorf, 1992).

Research Question 6: How reliant are the students on their teacher? (20, 21)

Although the students attach at least some value to the feedback they receive from peers, only about 4% of students from both groups stated that they preferred getting feedback from their peers to getting feedback from their teacher (see Table 5, Q.20); however, the MBA students seem to be slightly less reliant on the teacher's feedback.

Judging by the students' reported expectation of a teacher's role, however, doing group work should be an acceptable mode of learning for these groups (see Table 5, Q.21). About 85% of the students from both groups stated they expect the teacher to guide them in gaining knowledge themselves rather than just provide them with the knowledge (spoon-feed them), a finding which contradicts Cortazzi and Jin's (1996) description of students' expectations of the teacher in China.

CONCLUSION — SHOULD WE CONTINUE TO USE GWTS WITH PRC STUDENTS?

There was no major objection to the use of GWTs among the PRC students who participated in the current study. In fact, a small majority of the younger, Group One students said they preferred group work to individual work, and there was even wider support for group work among the Group Two students. These fairly positive attitudes towards group work support the findings of Flowerdew (1998) and Roskams (1999) who studied Hong Kong students, and Meyer (1999) who observed Singaporean students. An even more positive reception to GWTs, particularly on the part of the younger learners, could be fostered by, firstly, helping them move away from their notions of individualistic, competitive education and reliance on the teacher, and, secondly, doing some consciousness-raising regarding the potential benefits of group work, and coaching in such areas as team building, time and task management. In addition, both groups of students said they expect the teacher to guide rather than just spoon-feed them.

If, then, the PRC students studied here deem group work to be a useful and enjoyable teaching methodology, and doing less teacher-centred work meets their expectations of a teacher's role, we can be more assured about the effectiveness of GWTs.

Regarding behaviour during GWTs, my findings seem to show that, as with the Singaporean students studied earlier (Meyer, 1999) we cannot necessarily base our expectations of PRC students' behaviour on the stereotypical Asian behaviours of prioritising group harmony and acting to save face. Many of my students seem to have beliefs and show behaviour more typical of the stereotypical forthright Westerner. This finding may be the result of China's increased openness to the West, and therefore the students' contact with Western culture before coming to Singapore. It may also be that the traditional stereotype of Chinese behaviour is too crude to provide good predictions of how Chinese students will behave in all specific contexts. This would coincide with what Littlewood (2000) concludes, that Asian students actually wish to behave (and do behave if given the chance) in ways which differ from the classroom behaviour norms they have been taught to follow.

If we possess this improved knowledge about the behavioural tendencies of our PRC students during a GWT, we can set our tasks, coach our students, and evaluate the product more appropriately and effectively. Given that my PRC students are more "Western" in their behaviour than expected, we can rely to some extent on the Western GWT practices of, for example peer reviewing and feedback. And we can act judiciously on the advice given in the wealth of Western-based group work research findings and group management guidelines, in administrating and evaluating our GWTs with PRC students. We must be careful to heed Littlewood's (1999:89) warning that stereotypes "distort reality in important ways ... and cannot serve as a firm basis for organizing ... pedagogy".

RECOMMENDATIONS FOR FUTURE RESEARCH

As the findings of this study contradict the traditional views of Chinese students and the findings of previous similar research, and are limited to just two groups of PRC students from one semester, there is a necessity for follow-up research to confirm and explain my findings. To discover if the findings are only specific to the cohort of students studied and the teachers involved, I would recommend an identical study be conducted on subsequent batches of students enrolled in the same programmes, but taught by teachers other than those involved in this study. However, to explore explanations for my unexpected findings, the study would need to be expanded to include the collection of student profiles and interviews with students regarding their previous learning experience and other possible influences on their attitudes.

REFERENCES

Anderson, P. V. (1985). What survey research tells us about writing at work. In L. Odell and D. Goswami (Eds.), *Writing in Non-academic Settings* (pp. 3–83). New York: Guilford.

Artemeva, N. & Logie, S. (2000). The Teaching and Practice of Peer Feedback in the Professional Communication Classroom: Introduction to Intellectual Teamwork. Paper presented at the Research and Practice in Professional Discourse Conference, City University of Hong Kong.

Battalio, J. (1993). The formal report project as shared-document collaboration: A plan for co-authorship. *Technical Communication Quarterly,* 2(2): 147–61.

Bosley, D. S. (1993). Cross-cultural collaboration: Whose culture is it anyway? *Technical Communication Quarterly,* 2(1): 51–62.

Brown, H. D. (1994). *Teaching by principles: An interactive approach to language pedagogy.* Englewood Cliffs, NJ: Prentice Hall Regents.

Bruffee, K. A. (1973). Collaborative learning: some practical models. *College English,* 34: 634–43.

—————— (1981). The structure of knowledge and the future of liberal education. *Liberal Education,* 67(1): 177–86.

Carson, J. G. & Nelson, G. L. (1994). Writing groups: Cross-cultural issues. *Journal of Second Language Writing,* 3(1): 17–30.

————— (1996). Chinese students' perceptions of ESL peer response group interaction. *Journal of Second Language Writing,* 5(1): 1–19.

Casari, L. E. & Povlacs, J. T. (1988). Practices in technical writing in agriculture and engineering industries, firms, and agencies. *Journal of Technical Writing and Communication,* 18(2): 143–59.

Cheng, W. & Warren, M. (1996). Hong Kong students' attitudes toward peer assessment in English language courses. *Asian Journal of English Language Teaching,* 6: 61–75.

Chu, L.; Chew, M. L. & Kitchen, T. (1997). How do we learn best? Preferences and strategies in learning and teaching styles at the National University of Singapore. *Language & Communication Review,* 1997 (1): 14–32.

Conway, R.; Kember, D.; Sivan, A. & Wu, M. (1993). Peer assessment of an individual's contribution to a group project. *Assessment and Evaluation in Higher Education,* 18(1): 45–56.

Cortazzi, M. & Jin, L. (1996). Cultures of learning: Language classrooms in China. In H. Coleman (Ed.), *Society and the Language Classroom* (pp. 169–206). Cambridge: Cambridge University Press.

Duin, A. H.; Jorn, L. A. & DeBower, M. S. (1991). Collaborative writing — courseware and telecommunications. In M. M. Lay & W. M. Karis (Eds.), *Collaborative Writing in Industry: Investigations in Theory and Practice* (pp. 146–69). Amityville, N.Y.: Baywood Publishing.

Faigley, L. & Miller, T. P. (1982). What we learn from writing on the job. *College English,* 44(4): 557–69.

Flowerdew, L. (1998). A culture-sensitive methodology for language teaching. Paper presented at the RELC Seminar, Singapore.

Garratt, L. (1995). Peer feedback in writing: Is it "culturally appropriate" for Hong Kong Chinese adult learner? *Occasional Papers in English Language Teaching, Chinese University of Hong Kong,* 5: 97–118.

Gudykunst, W. B. & Hammer, M. R. (1983). Basic training design: approaches to intercultural training. In D. Landis & R.W. Brislin (Eds.), *Handbook of Intercultural Training: Issues in Theory and Design, Vol. 1* (pp. 322–43). New York: Pergamon.

Johnson, D. W. & Johnson, R. T. (1993). What we know about cooperative learning at the college level. *Cooperative Learning,* 13(3): 17–18.

Killingsworth, M. J. & Jones, B. G. (1989). Division of labor or integrated teams: A crux in the management of technical communication? *Technical Communication,* 36(3): 210–21.

Littlewood, W. (1999). Defining and developing autonomy in East Asian contexts. *Applied Linguistics,* 20(1): 71–94.

Littlewood, W. (2000). Do Asian students really want to listen and obey? *ELT Journal,* 54(1): 31–36.

Lockhart, C. & Ng, P. (1993). How useful is peer response? *Perspectives* (Working papers of the Department of English, City Polytechnic of Hong Kong), 5(1): 17–29.

Mangelsdorf, K. (1992). Peer reviews in the ESL composition classroom: What do students think? *ELT Journal*, 46(3): 274–83.

Meyer, J. E. (1999). Group writing projects at the National University of Singapore: Student feedback. *Language & Communication Review*, 1999 (1): 24–33.

Morgan, M. & Murray, M. (1991). Insight and collaborative writing. In M. M. Lay & W. M. Karis (Eds.), *Collaborative Writing in Industry: Investigations in Theory and Practice* (pp. 64–81). Amityville, N.Y.: Baywood Publishing.

Nelson, G. (1995). Cultural differences in learning styles. In J. Reid (Ed.), *Learning Styles in the ESL Classroom* (pp. 3–18). Boston: Heinle & Heinle.

Reither, J. A. (1993). Bridging the gap: Scenic motives for collaborative writing in workplace and school. In R. Spilka (Ed.), *Writing in the Workplace: New Research Perspectives* (pp. 195–206). Carbondale and Edwardsville, IL: Southern Illinois University Press.

Roskams, T. (1999). Chinese EFL students' attitudes to peer feedback and peer assessment in an extended pairwork setting. *RELC Journal*, 30(1): 79–123.

Scott, A. M. (1988). Group projects in technical writing courses. *The Technical Writing Teacher*, 15(2): 138–42.

Shirk, H. N. (1991). Collaborative editing: A combination of peer and hierarchical editing techniques. In M. M. Lay & W. M. Karis (Eds.), *Collaborative Writing in Industry: Investigations in Theory and Practice* (pp. 242–61). Amityville, N.Y.: Baywood Publishing.

Stebbins, C. (1995). Culture-specific perceptual-learning-style preferences of postsecondary students of English as a second language. In J. Reid (Ed.), *Learning Styles in the ESL Classroom* (pp. 108–117). Boston: Heinle & Heinle.

Tebeaux, E. (1991). The shared-document collaborative case response: teaching and research implications of an in-house teaching strategy. In M. M. Lay & W. M. Karis (Eds.), *Collaborative Writing in Industry: Investigations in Theory and Practice* (pp. 124–45). Amityville, N.Y.: Baywood Publishing.

Trimbur, J. (1989). Consensus and difference in collaborative learning. *College English*, 51(6): 602–616.

Van Pelt, W. & Gillam, A. (1991). Peer collaboration and the computer-assisted classroom: bridging the gap between academia and the workplace. In M. M. Lay & W. M. Karis (Eds.), *Collaborative Writing in Industry: Investigations in Theory and Practice* (pp. 170–205). Amityville, N.Y.: Baywood Publishing.

Voloshinov, V. N. (1986). *Marxism and the philosophy of language*. Matejka, L. M. & Titunik, I. R. (Trans). Cambridge, MA: Harvard University Press.

Weiss, T. (1991). Bruffee, the Bakhtin circle, and the concept of collaboration. In M. M. Lay and W. M. Karis (Eds.), *Collaborative Writing in Industry: Investigations in Theory and Practice* (pp. 31–48). Amityville, N.Y.: Baywood Publishing.

Wickliff, G. A. (1997). Assessing the value of client-based group projects in an introductory technical communication course. *Journal of Business and Technical Communication*, 11(2): 170–91.

Zhang, S. (1995). Re-examining the affective advantage of peer feedback in the ESL writing class. *Journal of Second Language Writing*, 4(3): 209–222.

APPENDIX A. GROUP WORK QUESTIONNAIRE

This questionnaire is being administered to help teachers at NUS learn more about the learning style preferences of their students. I would appreciate it if you would answer the following questions as honestly as you can.

1. Generally, which do you feel is more enjoyable?
   Group work ___ individual work ___

2. Generally, in most cases, which do you value more highly?
   The group (any group you belong to) ___
   the individual (yourself) ___
   hard to say ___

3. According to Confucian tradition, students learn through co-operation, by working for the common good, and by not elevating themselves above others. Would you say you learn this way?
   Yes ___ No ___   Can't say ___

4. It has been said that in many Asian societies each person must be part of a group or community, co-operating together. Would you say this is true in your own case?
   Generally yes ___ Generally no___

5. If you are working in a group on a project how do you measure your success/ achievement? (tick as many as are applicable)
   ___ the amount you've contributed to the group's welfare
   ___ how much you've helped to maintain group harmony
   ___ how much you've contributed to the final product
   ___ how outspoken you've been (how actively you have participated)
   ___ how many good ideas you've contributed

6. It has been said that confrontation in group work is limited to middle-class Euro-North American culture. How common would you say confrontation is in groups you've worked with?
   ___ There's **never** any confrontation.
   ___ Confrontation is **rare**.
   ___ There is **sometimes** confrontation.
   ___ Confrontation is **common**.

7. In your viewpoint is confrontation in group work acceptable?
   Generally no ___   Generally yes ___

8. If you're working in a group on a project, do you ever make a statement or agree with others in your group to maintain group harmony, even if it's not what you personally believe?
    Never _____ seldom _____ sometimes _____ often _____

9. If another group member asks you if you agree about a point being discussed, and you don't agree, do you:
    Respond with a definite no? _____
    Disagree tactfully? _____
    Say you agree anyway, just to maintain group harmony? _____
    Say you agree anyway, just to get the work done more quickly? _____

10. If another group member asks you to take on more work in the project and you don't feel you should do more do you:
    Respond with a definite no? _____
    Decline tactfully? _____
    Say you'll do it anyway, just to maintain group harmony? _____
    Say you'll do it anyway, just to get the work done more quickly? _____

11. If you're working on a project with a group, and there's something about the project you don't understand do you admit you don't understand and/or ask for clarification?
    Never _____ seldom _____ sometimes _____ often _____

12. If there is someone in your group who is either not doing his or her fair share, or is doing poor or inappropriate work do you complain about or criticise that person or his/her work?
    Yes _____ No, to avoid embarrassing him/her _____
    No, to get the work done faster _____

13. If you feel there's something additional which needs to be done in the project, or that something that has already been done could be done more creatively or better, do you point this out to the group?
    No, because I just want to get the project done as quickly as possible. _____
    No, because I don't want to risk making a foolish suggestion. _____
    Yes. _____

14. Do you feel comfortable when others in your group compliment your work?
    Yes _____   No _____

15. Do you feel comfortable with receiving feedback from your group-mates about your work?
    No problem _____
    a little uncomfortable _____
    definitely uncomfortable _____

16. Do you value the feedback on your work given to you by your group-mates?
    Yes, greatly ____ Yes, somewhat ____ not really ____

17. Do you feel comfortable with receiving feedback from classmates (not members of your group) about your work?
    No problem ____ a little uncomfortable ____
    definitely uncomfortable ___

18. Do you value the feedback on your work given to you by your classmates (not members of your group)?
    Yes, greatly ____ Yes, somewhat ____ not really ____

19. Do you feel comfortable with giving feedback to another group about their work?
    No problem ____ a little uncomfortable ____
    Definitely uncomfortable ____

20. Generally, do you prefer getting feedback on your work from your classmates or your teacher?
    Classmates ____ tutor ____ no preference (equal) ____

21. In your English class here at NUS which do you expect your teachers to do more of:
    give you knowledge? ___ or
    guide you in gaining the knowledge yourself? ___

CHAPTER 6

"You Dig Tree Tree to NUS": Understanding Singapore English from the Perspectives of International Students

CARISSA YOUNG

INTRODUCTION

Zhao (pseudonym), a student from the People's Republic of China, told the author the following story:

> The first week of my stay in Singapore was awful. Once I wanted to go to the university but I lost my way, so I asked a man for direction. "You dig tree tree to NUS lah", said the man. I looked around and saw many trees, but I didn't know why he told me to dig up a tree. Fortunately this good-hearted Singaporean walked me to the bus stop and pointed at a coming bus, which was bus service No. 33.... I used to think that Singaporeans speak like Americans but they don't. I was disappointed.

Like Zhao, other Chinese students taking an intensive English course at the National University of Singapore have told the author that they have difficulties understanding the English language used by Singaporeans. It would appear that they do not know that the English used by Singaporeans is different from other varieties of English in the world. In order to understand these newly arrived international students' attitudes towards the English Language in Singapore, the author conducted the questionnaire study described in this chapter.

The English Language in Singapore

English has been the official language of Singapore since this island became a British colony in 1819. Although Chinese, Malay and Tamil gained their official status when Singapore declared her independence in 1965, English still remains the most important language of this country. Singaporeans generally conceive English as the tool of business communication and the common language among the Indian, Malay and Chinese racial groups in Singapore. According to the Singapore Department of Statistics (2001), among the literate population, literacy in English increased from 62.8% in 1990 to 70.9% in 2000. Such increase "is partly due to the adoption of English as the main medium of instruction in schools and partly due to the use of English as the working language for administration and business" (Singapore Department of Statistics, 2001: 2).

In this chapter, the term *Singapore English* refers to the variety of English used by Singaporeans (Brown, 2000). Singapore English has received much research attention and the categorisation of this variety of English has been a controversial topic. However, since categorisation is not the main interest of this paper, the author would like to take up Gupta's (1994) diglossic view of Singapore English, which involves a "high variety" and a "low variety" of Singapore English.

According to Gupta, *Standard Singapore English*, or the "high variety", is used in formal circumstances such as public speeches, lectures and international communications. The written form of Standard Singapore English can usually be understood by other speakers of English, as Gupta asserts that Standard Singapore English and other Standard Englishes are different only in terms of the phonological features and some culture specific lexical terms. On the other hand, *Colloquial Singapore English*, or the "low variety" of Singapore English, is used in informal circumstances such as conversations among family members and friends. Used mainly in its spoken form, Colloquial Singapore English has been influenced by Malay, Tamil as well as Southern Chinese dialects such as Hokkien, Teochew and Cantonese (Ho and Platt, 1993). According to some specialists (Gupta, 1994; Bao, 1998), the phonological, lexical as well as syntactical features of Colloquial Singapore English are very different from those of Standard Singapore English and other varieties of English.

Some studies have viewed Singapore English from the perspectives of Singaporeans. According to Lim (1986), many Singaporeans regard Singapore English as a national identity of Singapore. By using the two local varieties of English, the subjects of this former British colony can distinguish themselves from those who use British English. Besides, young Singaporeans use the low variety to enhance personal intimacy. In theory, the highly-educated Singaporeans know both the high and low varieties of Singapore English and they use these varieties of English "appropriately". Students would use the low variety when they speak to a toilet attendant (who only knows the low variety), or write to their peers. They would "switch" to the high variety when they speak to their tutors or write their term papers. In practice, however, some highly-educated people might use the low variety of Singapore English even in formal situations. The results of another study (Saravanan and Poedjosoedarmo, 1997) suggest that some teachers are positive about the use of Colloquial Singapore English in the classroom.

The Purposes of the Present Study

Although much effort has been made in studying Singaporeans' language attitudes, at the time when this study was designed, little effort has been made to examine Singapore English from the perspectives of international students. Yet this neglected area should be explored. Since international students may not know about the existence of the high and low varieties of Singapore English as linguists do, their attitudes towards the English used in this country may be negatively affected. This study aimed to investigate Chinese students' attitudes towards the English used by Singaporeans and to determine whether or not these students' attitudes towards Singapore English would change over time. The questions explored in this study were (1) "What were the Chinese students' attitudes towards Singapore English when they arrived in Singapore?" and (2) "Would the Chinese students' attitudes towards Singapore English change significantly over time?"

The results of this study should help language teachers better understand their international students' opinions about the use of English in multicultural classrooms and become more aware of the communication problems that their language students might have in cross-cultural communications.

METHOD

The subjects of this study totalled 193 (148 males, 45 females) pre-university students from the People's Republic of China. Their average age was 18. These students had been learning English as a foreign language for six years before they were enrolled in an intensive English course conducted by the National University of Singapore under the auspices of the Singapore Ministry of Education. They took this 6-month intensive English course to prepare themselves for undergraduate studies. These students belonged to 10 tutorial groups, each of which comprised 19 or 20 students. They had English classes 30 hours a week from December 1998 to early June 1999.

A direct attitude questionnaire of 21 items (Appendix A) was designed by the author, who was a tutor of the English course. The questionnaire attempted to measure these students' attitudes towards the English language used in Singapore and their reasons for learning English in Singapore. The questionnaire asked the students to rate 21 statements about Singapore English such as "English spoken by Singaporeans is easy to understand". To avoid any neutral responses, a four-point Likert-scale ranging from "strongly agree" ("1") to "strongly disagree" ("4") was used to obtain a positive or negative response.

To find out whether there were any attitude changes, the questionnaire was administered twice at a 5-month interval. The same questionnaire was used in the two data collection sessions. The students answered the questionnaire administered by their English tutors during class periods in mid-December 1998 (Week 3 of the course, when students had had some contact with Singaporeans) and late May 1999 (Week 25, before the final tests). They were instructed that the questionnaire aimed to examine their attitudes towards the English used in Singapore. They were told that the information collected from them would be analysed anonymously and used for research purposes only. They were asked to read the statements carefully and rate the extent to which they agreed with each statement. Most of the students completed the questionnaire within 15 minutes.

The information collected from the two data-gathering sessions was analysed using the statistical package *SPSS for Windows 9.0*. The means and standard deviations of each of the 21 items were calculated. To determine whether or not there were significant attitude changes,

Paired-samples t-tests[1] were performed to compare the students' ratings of the same item at two different times. Since there was no previous empirical evidence for differences in these means or for directionality, a null hypothesis of no significant differences in means between the first and the second administration of the questionnaire was adopted. The level of significance was set at $\alpha < 0.05$, non-directional.

RESULTS AND DISCUSSION

Chinese Students' Attitudes Towards the English Language in Singapore

To answer Research Question One: "What were the Chinese students' attitudes towards Singapore English when they arrived in Singapore?", the students' responses to the first administration of the questionnaire are presented. As shown in Table 1, the Chinese students agreed with the following statements most when they answered the questionnaire for the first time:

> Statement 4: "Singaporeans should learn American or British English" ($mean_1 = 1.93$).

> Statement 18: "If I know Singapore English, I will understand the Singaporeans and their culture" ($mean_1 = 2.02$).

> Statement 21: "The quality of English used by Singaporean TV news presenters is high" ($mean_1 = 2.02$).

The respondents agreed most with Statement 4 "Singaporeans should learn American or British English" ($mean_1 = 1.93$). In fact, it is not surprising to find that these Chinese students preferred North American or British English to Singapore English because North American and British English were the only varieties they had ever known. According to Zhao and Campbell (1995), several English teaching programmes have been aired in China for many years by BBC and Radio Canada

---

[1]The use of t-tests on the data should be interpreted with extra caution because a Likert-scale is not an interval scale in its strictest sense.

Table 1. Results of Paired-samples t-tests on the Mean Differences Between the First and Second Administration of the Questionnaire

Statements	1st Adm. Mean$_1$#(SD)	2nd Adm. Mean$_2$#(SD)	t value
1. Singapore English is the symbol of an uneducated person.	2.97 (0.64)	3.03 (0.70)	−1.19
2. English written by Singaporeans is easy to understand.	2.46 (0.57)	2.40 (0.65)	1.01
3. English spoken by Singaporeans is easy to understand.	3.14 (0.70)	2.80 (0.74)	5.32**
4. Singaporeans should learn American or British English.	1.93 (0.68)	2.28 (0.87)	−4.93**
5. As long as it is understood, incorrect English is acceptable.	2.47 (0.74)	2.31 (0.66)	2.55*
6. I prefer friends from USA or UK to those from Singapore.	2.89 (0.77)	3.00 (0.79)	−1.64
7. I am interested in the English of Singapore.	2.69 (0.73)	2.66 (0.71)	0.45
8. If I use Singapore English, my local friends and classmates will accept me.	2.28 (0.71)	2.19 (0.71)	1.22
9. I study English because it is required for graduation.	2.75 (0.86)	2.84 (0.80)	−1.29
10. I like to listen to local English radio channels.	2.48 (0.69)	2.39 (0.71)	1.33
11. Studying English in Singapore is enjoyable.	2.13 (0.73)	2.30 (0.65)	2.91**
12. If I speak Singapore English, people will think I am not well educated.	3.01 (0.65)	3.06 (0.58)	−0.86
13. Singaporeans can write accurate English.	2.09 (0.50)	2.08 (0.61)	0.22

(cont'd overleaf)

Table 1. *(cont'd)*

Statements	1st Adm. Mean₁#(SD)	2nd Adm. Mean₂#(SD)	t value
14. Singaporeans can speak correct English.	2.45 (0.68)	2.23 (0.65)	3.80**
15. Unlike American or British English, Singapore English is a non-standard language.	2.30 (0.63)	2.46 (0.66)	–2.36*
16. Even if I make mistakes in English, people will still understand what I mean.	2.07 (0.56)	2.04 (0.47)	0.49
17. I do not like to make friends with Singaporeans.	3.58 (0.58)	3.48 (0.65)	1.93
18. If I know Singapore English, I will understand the Singaporeans and their culture.	2.02 (0.75)	2.10 (0.71)	–1.33
19. I think that by using Singapore English I will feel like a Singaporean.	2.70 (0.72)	2.62 (0.78)	1.08
20. I learn English in Singapore because I want to work here.	2.66 (0.73)	2.68 (0.61)	–0.36
21. The quality of English used by Singaporean TV news presenters is high.	2.02 (0.60)	1.93 (0.63)	1.49

Notes: * $p < 0.05$ (2-tailed), ** $p < 0.01$ (2-tailed)
\# The smaller the mean score, the more the respondents agreed with the statement.

International. However, to the best knowledge of the author, no Singapore English programmes have ever been broadcast on Chinese television or radio. Since the students learned American or British English when they were in China, they thought that Singaporeans should also learn these popular varieties of English.

The Chinese students disagreed with the following statements most:

Statement 17: "I do not like to make friends with Singaporeans" (mean₁ = 3.58).

Statement 3: "English spoken by Singaporeans is easy to understand" (mean$_1$ = 3.14).

Statement 12: "If I speak Singapore English, people will think I am not well educated" (mean$_1$ = 3.01).

It is noted that the respondents only disagreed or strongly disagreed with Statement 3 "English spoken by Singaporeans is easy to understand" (mean$_1$ = 3.14) but not Statement 2 "English written by Singaporeans is easy to understand" (mean$_1$ = 2.46), which implies that these Chinese students had negative attitudes only towards the spoken English of the local people. A possible interpretation of this result is that these Chinese students have more opportunities to listen to Singaporeans, who usually use Colloquial Singapore English in informal conversations. For example, these Chinese students might have heard local students chatting at the canteen. However, these students might have read the local English newspapers or teaching materials prepared by their English tutors only, which are all constructed in standard English. They might not have read Singaporeans' English on informal occasions, which could be written in other varieties of Singapore English since educated English-speakers in Singapore could shift between Standard and Colloquial Singapore English (Lim, 1986; Gupta, 1994). For instance, if the local students would like to communicate with these Chinese students, they would probably use a more "standard" form of English other than the colloquial variety they would prefer to use among peers. Therefore, it is not surprising that the Chinese students did not have negative attitudes towards the English written by Singaporeans.

If these Chinese students had relatively negative attitudes towards the English language in Singapore, why did they come to Singapore to learn English? Would they like to learn Singapore English? The answers to the above questions can be seen from their responses to the following statements:

Statement 18: "If I know Singapore English, I will understand the Singaporeans and their culture" (mean$_1$ = 2.02).

Statement 8: "If I use Singapore English, my local friends and classmates will accept me" (mean$_1$ = 2.28).

Statement 10: "I study English because it is required for graduation" ($\text{mean}_1 = 2.48$).

Statement 20: "I learn English in Singapore because I want to work here" ($\text{mean}_1 = 2.66$).

It can be argued that these Chinese students studied English in Singapore probably because English is widely used in university and the work place (Statements 10 and 20). However, the surveyed Chinese students did not seem to reject the local variety of English as they agreed that a command of Singapore English would help them know the Singapore culture. They also realised that the function of Singapore English was mainly to communicate with their local classmates and friends. These findings are consistent with the results of a previous study that Singapore English is a national identity of Singaporeans, and that this unique variety of English is used to enhance personal intimacy (Lim, 1986).

Chinese Students' Attitudinal Changes Towards Singapore English

To answer Research Question Two: "Would the Chinese students' attitudes towards Singapore English change significantly over time?", the results of the two administrations of the questionnaire were compared using *Paired-samples t-Tests*. It was found that there were significant differences in some of the mean scores between the first and second administration of the questionnaire (Table 1).

Regarding the spoken English used by Singaporeans, the mean scores of Statement 3, "English spoken by Singaporeans is easy to understand" ($\text{mean}_1 = 3.14$, $\text{mean}_2 = 2.80$, $t = 5.32$, $p < 0.01$) were significantly different at the 0.01 level. As mentioned above, the respondents disagreed or strongly disagreed with this statement when they answered the questionnaire at the beginning of the course. However, the lower mean score in the second administration of the questionnaire indicated that they changed their minds and these Chinese students clearly became more positive. Besides, a significant mean difference was shown in the students' responses to Statement 14, "Singaporeans can speak correct English" ($\text{mean}_1 = 2.45$, $\text{mean}_2 = 2.23$, $t = 3.80$, $p < 0.01$), implying that these students began to realise that the spoken English of Singaporeans is not incorrect English.

It is interesting to note that the students' attitudes towards the written English used by Singaporeans did not show any significant changes over time. The mean scores of Statement 13,' "Singaporeans can write accurate English" ($mean_1 = 2.09$, $mean_2 = 2.08$) were almost identical. Similarly, little mean difference was shown in Statement 2, "English written by Singaporeans is easy to understand" ($mean_1 = 2.46$, $mean_2 = 2.40$). Again it is possible that the students had more access to Singaporeans' spoken English than their written English.

As for the students' opinions of Singapore English and American/British English, significant mean differences were found in Statement 4, "Singaporeans should learn American or British English" ($mean_1 = 1.93$, $mean_2 = 2.28$, $t = -4.93$, $p < 0.01$) as well as Statement 15, "Unlike American or British English, Singapore English is a non-standard language ($mean_1 = 2.30$, $mean_2 = 2.46$, $t = -2.36$, $p < 0.05$). The mean scores indicated that fewer Chinese students agreed with these statements, showing that they began to regard Singapore English as another variety of English. They realised that Singapore English was not worse than other varieties such as American or British English. One possible reason for the attitudinal change is that these students had more contact with the local people.

TEACHING IMPLICATIONS

The results of this questionnaire study clearly show that initially the Chinese students had relatively negative attitudes towards the spoken form of Singapore English. It would seem that these students did not know much about the different varieties of English in the world and how spoken English is used in real life. Their lack of knowledge might make it difficult for these students to adjust themselves to the new language environment. The findings support the view that the education system in China focuses more on the importance of examinations than students' communication ability (Zhao & Campbell, 1995). To polish Chinese students' English communication skills, it is recommended that the language teachers in China would do well to take time to clarify precisely what varieties English has and how these varieties are different from one another. Language teachers who have access to the Internet could use online teaching materials with audio files of world Englishes. In this way, those Chinese students who are planning to further their studies in Singapore would have an opportunity to listen to this new and yet unfamiliar variety of English before leaving home.

The survey results also indicated that the Chinese students' attitudes towards Singapore English changed gradually. This is probably because these Chinese students had better communication with the local people. To accelerate this process, language teachers in Singapore could design language materials or activities to help the Chinese students familiarise themselves with the variety of English used by Singaporeans. They could play a local TV programme in class and explain the meanings of some Colloquial Singapore English expressions to their international students. In a multicultural classroom, the language teacher could design a language game for their local and Chinese students. They could have one local student read aloud a sentence in Colloquial Singapore English and have a Chinese student translate it into Standard English. The advantages of this game are that the Chinese students would know more about the English used by Singaporeans in informal situations and that the local Singaporean students would be more aware of the problems that the use of Colloquial Singapore English might bring in international communication.

Finally, it was found that some Chinese students might have problems comprehending the low variety of Singapore English. Therefore, the author suggests that teachers refrain from using Colloquial Singapore English in class. Although some teachers prefer to use Colloquial Singapore English to explain some concepts to their Singaporean students (Saravanan and Poedjosoedarmo, 1997), they should know that international students such as those from China would not understand what they mean. Therefore, there may be advantages in using the high variety of English as often as possible.

CONCLUSIONS

To conclude this paper, the author would like to cite an email message from Lin (pseudonym), who participated in this survey:

> Actually I realised one "mistake" I made when I filled in the questionnaire. The statement was "If I use Singapore English, my local friends and classmates will accept me." At that time, I chose the "Disagree" option. But now if I were given a second chance,

I would tick "Agree" or even "Strongly Agree". I have no explanation for such an answer. It was derived from my experience and what the Singaporeans told me.

The above message shows us that some Chinese students like Lin might one day become very positive towards the use of Singapore English. A more distinct difference might be seen if the same questionnaire was administered after a longer period of time; further research in this respect would be welcome. Alternatively, a longitudinal case study of individual students could reveal their changes of attitudes towards Singapore English. The present study has focused on Chinese students and examined their opinions on Singapore English; however, it will be equally interesting to survey students from other nations so that a more comprehensive view of international students' attitudes towards Singapore English could be obtained.

REFERENCES

Brown, A. (2000). *Singapore English in a Nutshell: An Alphabetical Description of Its Features.* Singapore: Federal Publications.

Bao, Z. M. (1998). The sounds of Singapore English. In J. A. Foley *et al.* (Eds.), *English in New Cultural Contexts: Reflections from Singapore* (pp. 152–74). Singapore: Oxford University Press.

Gupta, A. F. (1994). A framework for the analysis of Singapore English. In S. Gopinathan, A. Pakir, W. K. Ho & V. Saravanan (Eds.), *Language, Society and Education in Singapore: Issues and Trends* (pp. 123–40). Singapore: Times Academic Press.

Ho, M. L. & Platt, J. T. (1993). *Dynamics of a Contact Continuum: Singapore English.* Oxford: Clarendon Press.

Lim, C. (1986). *English in Singapore: A Study of Its Status and Solidarity and the Attitudes to Its Use.* Unpublished doctoral dissertation, National University of Singapore, Singapore.

Saravanan, V. & Poedjosoedarmo, G. R. (1997). An exploration of attitudes towards various models of English pronunciation among Singaporean teachers: some methodological considerations. In A. Brown (Ed.), *English in Southeast Asia 96: Proceedings of the First 'English in Southeast Asia' Conference held at the National Institute of Education, Singapore 21–23 November 1996* (pp. 67–79). Singapore: National Institute of Education.

Singapore Department of Statistics (2001). *Singapore Census of Population 2000 Advance Data Release No. 3.* Singapore: Census of Population Office.

Zhao, Y. & Campbell, K. P. (1995). English in China. *World Englishes,* 14(3): 377–90.

APPENDIX A. THE QUESTIONNAIRE USED IN THE PRESENT STUDY

Chinese Students' Attitudes Towards Singapore English

This questionnaire examines your attitudes towards Singapore English. All the data collected from this survey will be used for research purposes only. Please answer **all** the questions truthfully.

Please tell us the extent to which you agree or disagree with the following statements. **Circle** the appropriate number using the scale below

1 = I *Strongly Agree* with this statement.
2 = I *Agree* with this statement.
3 = I *Disagree* with this statement.
4 = I *Strongly Disagree* with this statement.

Statements	Responses
1. Singapore English is the symbol of an uneducated person.	1 2 3 4
2. English written by Singaporeans is easy to understand.	1 2 3 4
3. English spoken by Singaporeans is easy to understand.	1 2 3 4
4. Singaporeans should learn American or British English.	1 2 3 4
5. As long as it is understood, incorrect English is acceptable.	1 2 3 4
6. I prefer friends from USA or UK to those from Singapore.	1 2 3 4
7 I am interested in the English of Singapore.	1 2 3 4
8. If I use Singapore English, my local friends and classmates will accept me.	1 2 3 4
9. I study English because it is required for graduation.	1 2 3 4
10. I like to listen to local English radio channels.	1 2 3 4
11. Studying English in Singapore is enjoyable.	1 2 3 4
12. If I speak Singapore English, people will think I am not well educated.	1 2 3 4
13. Singaporeans can write accurate English.	1 2 3 4
14. Singaporeans can speak correct English.	1 2 3 4
15. Unlike American or British English, Singapore English is a non-standard language.	1 2 3 4
16. Even if I make mistakes in English, people will still understand what I mean.	1 2 3 4
17. I do not like to make friends with Singaporeans.	1 2 3 4
18. If I know Singapore English, I will understand the Singaporeans and their culture.	1 2 3 4
19. I think that by using Singapore English I will feel like a Singaporean.	1 2 3 4
20. I learn English in Singapore because I want to work here.	1 2 3 4
21. The quality of English used by Singaporean TV news presenters is high.	1 2 3 4

CHAPTER 7

Is the Oral Strip Story Suitable for ESL/EFL Students to Experience Real Communication?

MOHLEEN CHEW

In teaching any group of ESL/EFL students, one difficult task I have is finding appropriate activities for students to practise real communication. Real communication is understood in the context of what Harvey (1982) says,

> "We want the language learner to learn to use the language. That's how he's going to learn to use it. But we have to be sure that he's really using it, not just appearing to use it." (p.205)

So, the challenge for me has always been the search for activities whereby students can creatively apply the language rules that they have learnt to form and to sustain meaningful utterances competently. Meaningful is used in the sense that students know the logic and the truth of what is being said.

One thing I believe about communication is this — it is a function of need and students should learn to speak unpretentiously with linguistic competence, which is the mastery of the sound system and the basic structural patterns of English as propounded by linguists like Chomsky (1969) and Stevick (1982). Believing this, I must then create a function and a need for students to listen and talk. One such functional need activity that I found constructive in providing protracted communication practice among ESL/EFL students is what I call — the "Oral Strip Story".

When a strip story is mentioned, perhaps the conventional image of students frantically putting strips of paper together to develop the story is conjectured. Indeed, in using this method for students to practise language competence, a common practice is this: language instructors would print the story on a piece of paper and cut out strips with each containing a sentence. Students in the class or group get all the jumbled strips in a whole pile and they are then instructed to read every sentence strip silently to understand its meaning and structure. Finally, as a joint effort, they build up the story by arranging each strip in a logical order.

The Oral Strip Story Technique

Gibson's Version

Using a strip story for oral communication was first proposed by Robert E. Gibson (Gibson, 1975), and he named it the "Strip Story". The preparation of Gibson's strip story is similar to the conventional technique in one step only; that is, the instructor prints the chosen story on paper and cuts out strips of paper with one sentence on one strip. The number of strips should correspond with the number of students in the group.

The strips are jumbled and placed in a basket. To participate in the task, students sit in a circle and each draws a strip randomly from the basket. They are then given a minute or two to memorise the sentence. The paper strips are taken away after that. With the memorised sentence, students are told to piece together the cut-up story through speaking only. They are not allowed to write at all. From then on, the instructor keeps quiet; s/he does not give any input as to how the story could be constructed, except to help students who are obviously baffled by difficulties in vocabulary or pronunciation. In this manner, students are forced to complete the task through speaking and listening only. When group members are satisfied with the description of their story, each takes turn to read aloud following the sentence sequence that the group has decided upon.

Researcher's Version

Gibson used the strip story exercise with just one group of students. Keeping the same manner of conducting the Gibson's strip story, I have, however, learned to alter the strip story task to playing a game between two to three groups of students and awarding a prize to the group that has the closest match to the original story. I had reasons to turn the oral strip story into a game. Games and prizes add excitement and fun to the task and together enhance participation and learning. Besides evoking fun and promoting enjoyable learning when a game is played, language use takes over language practice in such a situation (Johnson, 1973). Moreover, the use of language in games is task oriented and this takes students closer to a real world of authentic communication.

Another change that I made to the strip story task was to instruct each group of students to write their completed story on overhead transparencies after they were satisfied with their oral version. The transparencies with the original story were simultaneously (or sequentially) projected on the walls so that all could read. Students were then asked to compare and contrast each group's version with the original version, and then to challenge one another. At this point, besides letting students argue over the winning version, I also guided the discussion to focus on my lessons in grammar, structure, pronunciation, and vocabulary.

The final difference is that Gibson used the strip story as a speaking and listening exercise only, whereas I extended the task to a written exercise, requiring students to submit a piece of writing using similar paragraph development employed in the given story.

I discovered that firstly, these alterations generated more communication among all the players than when the strip story task was done by just one group of students. This is chiefly because in the case of the strip story game being played by two to three groups of students, all of them were able to study what the other groups had to offer when the various versions were reflected on the overhead projector. And when challenged about their group's version of the story, the group members had to defend it, thus encouraging further communication. Additionally, I had the opportunity to correct or teach the intended grammar points, pronunciation, and vocabulary. Lastly, the writing task gave students a chance to recognise the pattern of paragraph development that they had learned before in this given strip story and subsequently practise using it.

To distinguish my version of the strip story both from Gibson's and the conventional one, I will call it the "Oral Strip Story" from now on.

Potential for Language Use, Learning, and Teaching

In using this activity, Gibson reported that students participated actively using real communication. I had similar experience whenever the oral strip story was used. By listening to the memorised sentences, by asking questions to clarify a pronunciation or meaning of a word, and by arguing about the logical sequence of the sentences, students themselves had much to learn and to teach each other about the various language skills.

The best part about using the oral strip story to teach is that the instructor has complete control over the language skill areas that s/he wants students to learn and practise. In choosing the story, the instructor considers how the activity can be stretched to teaching certain grammatical points, to addressing certain pronunciation problems, to enlarging certain vocabulary, and to writing certain patterns of paragraph development. For instance, in teaching a group of intermediate ESL Chinese students who tended to ignore the use of appropriate transitional elements in their writing and speaking, and who had difficulties differentiating "while" and "well", I chose an Aesop fable entitled *The Thief and The Boy* (see Appendix A), whereby students had to consider the meaning and use of transitional elements and to pronounce the mentioned words in order to produce a story close to the original. Also, to be in line with the university's policy to encourage creativity among students, such a story with a twist was chosen to influence students to deduce and infer imaginatively. Furthermore, I wanted them to creatively craft a moral teaching point in the story they had to write.

Researcher's Observations

When a group of ESL/EFL students were told that they could not write what they had memorised but use other means to piece the story strips together, there was initially embarrassed silence. However, very quickly without prompting, someone would say something like, "Why don't we say our sentences out loud? I'll start." Subsequently, students would initiate group work and discussions and actively interact with one another in English, gestures, and their first language, Chinese, to propose and reject the order of the story strips.

Real Communication

The communication process within and between groups was spontaneous and energetic, allowing everyone, even the reticent ones, to use English uninhibitedly. A case in point was a student who just recited his sentence once when it was his turn to do so, and thereafter slipped into introversion. His group members had somehow forgotten him and were arranging their sentences in a chronological order; when he saw that, he blurted out "What about my sentence?" Thus, he had to repeat his sentence and be involved in the formation of the story.

Occasionally, when students got excited, they switched to their first language. That was not corrected or penalised in any way as I felt that any correction/penalty would raise the anxiety level and disrupt the rapport that students had with one another, which might lead to a disruption of their train of thought and thereby hamper their progress in the story building (Auerbach, 1993). The switch to their first language was at most minimal because they always had to revert to the memorised sentences in English.

Some may question whether students have any real language practice in memorising and repeating sentences that someone else has created. In an oral strip story activity, players do not mindlessly repeat what they have memorised; they have a meaningful task to expound — to fashion the stripped sentences in a logical manner. In fact, memorising the sentence is a positive learning feature of the oral strip story as students can emulate the memorised sentence structure for future language use. Considering this, the memorised text then serves as a springboard to help students use the language for themselves to complete the task rather than as a means of parroting the text. In a sense, students are armed with a structured sentence, yet at the same time they need to use the language functionally to communicate their questions, suggestions, and disagreements. To a certain extent, the activity embodies the characteristic features of communicative language learning whereby students pay attention to functional as well as structural aspects of the target language (Littlewood, 1981).

Speaking, Listening, Vocabulary, and Pronunciation

Within each group, it was observed that players had no choice but to interact with one another actively as each had to play his/her part in constructing the story; so each must listen intently and actively to other links in the story. In turn, each was encouraged to speak clearly, audibly and boldly to get his/her sentence and ideas across.

Noticeable among members of the same group was peer learning with regard to pronunciation and meanings of words. For instance, a student questioned the meaning of the word "mug" in the story, *The Thief and The Boy*; the person with the word spelled it. Yet another team-mate tried to explain it in English or in his/her first language, and a third person used gestures to describe the object. One student pronounced, "well" as /waɪl/. Acknowledging some puzzled looks, the speaker spelled the word and one response was, "Oh, you mean /wel/." To which, the speaker replied, "Yes, that's what I meant, /wel/." It was surprising how quickly they each corrected one another, when I had difficulty correcting their vowel differentiations of "while" /waɪl/, "well"/wel/, and "wail"/weɪl/.

Between different groups, students inclined to be argumentative and defensive about their versions of the completed story. This is another positive feature of the oral strip story as it spawned increasingly genuine exchange of information. Actually, the rebuttals and debates were so swiftly executed that the majority of the students who were in the habit of translating what they heard and uttered into their first language had the least opportunity to do so in such rapid exchange in the target language.

Creative Thinking and Writing

The students' imagination was stretched while juggling the possible permutations of the sentence strips. A group that started with three protagonists while attempting to arrange the strips in the story, *The Thief and The Boy*, ended up with two — just the boy and the thief — as they delved into the sentences and understood the connections better. Carefully chosen, the story could be used to promote students' thinking skills in deductions and inferences. While participating in the task, students had to deal with all the verbalised English sentences in their minds before they could offer their views; so they were thinking and speaking in English.

When students were asked to write a story with a moral teaching point using similar paragraph development in the strip story, some came up with stories that they had read or heard before. So, stories like *The Boy and The Wolf, The Bird, The Nest,* and *A Wooden Bowl* were widespread in which the characters themselves learned a maxim in life (see Appendix B.1). Others were more creative in concocting stories of their own experience. One gave a moral point about not cheating with experimental data by recounting a story of her classmate who cheated and failed consequently. Another fashioned a moral at the end of the story in the form of a question, "If you never care about other people, how can you expect others willing to help you?" (see Appendix B.2).

Whether it was a story written with original or unoriginal ideas, the goal was for students to use what they had discussed and learnt in the oral strip story and extend it to writing in English using the same kind of paragraph development. Some students seemed to have acquired certain sentence patterns, thought patterns, and words. One particular student used such sentences as, "It's just dandy for me to climb this tree" and "So he climbed down the tree, and he saw the boy and his watermelon were all gone!" (see Appendix B.3). Clearly, the structure and the words used had been transferred from the strip story, *The Thief and The Boy.*

Grammar and Structure

Of particular interest to me was the use of transitional elements because students were not consciously using them in their writing and oral presentations. *The Thief and The Boy* employs two commonly used transitional elements — "so after a while" and "therefore". In the course of organising the sentence strips, students were more concerned in lining up the ideas rather than considering language use. Thus, groups that did not pay attention to the use of transition elements were inclined to put the sentence with the word "therefore" before the sentence with the phrase "so after a while" (see Appendix C.1), sequence of which deviated from the original story. This different ordering of transitional elements resulted in students arguing why and how each element was used in linking the story strips. It was also an opportune time for me to emphasise the use of transitional elements in both speaking and writing.

Students who had memorised their sentences well were fluent in reciting grammatically and structurally correct sentences. Those who did not took a longer time to recite the sentences, and were inclined to compensate for their inadequacies by adding, deleting or changing parts of the sentences. Some of the changed sentences were inaccurate in structure, grammar, and meaning (see Appendix C.2), which delayed the group in forming the story quickly. This seemed to frustrate some players, but somehow, they tried to improvise with whatever they had heard. This observation reminded me to stress the need for each player to memorise the sentence well and to be involved in teamwork at the beginning of the game.

Students' Feedback

I am enthusiastic about the positive learning experience that students can get out of an oral strip story, but what do students actually think of the exercise? To get finer details of their learning experience, 86 intermediate ESL students from China at the National University of Singapore were asked to respond to this survey question, "In completing the strip story on *The Thief and The Boy*, to what extent do you agree that you have used or learnt more about the following English language skills?" (see Appendix D). The results are as follows:

Extent of Using/Learning English in Speaking and Listening

Speaking clearly and audibly was a primary requirement of every participant or else the oral strip story game could not proceed smoothly and successfully. A large percentage (83.7%) of students agreed that they had to do this so that others could hear their sentences (see Table 1). In addition, they had to speak out boldly or else they could not participate in the discussion to get the story right; students recognised the importance of this, as seen from the high agreement rate of 86.1%. Players were also aware of the necessity to listen to each other actively and attentively before they could form the story as a group, and this is reflected by 96.6% of the students.

During the exercise, it was clear that some students did not pronounce a few words clearly and correctly, for example, "well" was pronounced as /waɪl/, "groped" as /grɒp/, and "silver" as /sɪvəl/. Then why is it that a considerable 23.3% of the students remained neutral, even

Table 1.   Extent of Using/Learning English in Speaking and Listening (n = 86)

Agreement / Language Skill	Strongly Agree (%)	Agree (%)	Neutral (%)	Disagree (%)	Strongly Disagree (%)
(a) Speak clearly & audibly	31.4	52.3	16.3	0	0
(b) Speak out boldly in a group	29.1	57.0	12.8	1.1	0
(c) Listen actively & attentively	41.9	54.7	3.4	0	0
(d) Use correct pronunciation	26.7	47.7	23.3	2.3	0

though the majority (74.4%) agreed (see Table 1) that they had learnt correct pronunciation of words? The possible explanations are firstly, the words might not be new to a number of students; secondly, those who could not pronounce the words were few; thirdly, all the respondents were of a homogeneous group from China and somehow they were accustomed to each other's pronunciations and could understand one another well. Finally, students also indicated that pronunciation was a skill that was difficult to correct in just one lesson.

Extent of Thinking and Writing Creatively in English

Though 59.3% of the respondents (see Table 2) agreed that the exercise helped them to think creatively, there were 39.6% who stayed neutral on this question. Only half (50%) were keen about the writing assignment. My observation about most students' attitude towards any writing exercise was — "Oh no!" — it was always deemed a more laborious task compared to a speaking or listening task. So, it is not surprising to see a less enthusiastic response rate to writing creatively.

Table 2.   Extent of Thinking and Writing Creatively in English (n = 86)

Agreement / Language Skill	Strongly Agree (%)	Agree (%)	Neutral (%)	Disagree (%)	Strongly Disagree (%)
(a) Think creatively	31.4	27.9	39.6	1.1	0
(b) Write creatively	16.3	33.7	46.5	3.5	0

Table 3. Extent of Using/Learning English Grammar, Structure and Vocabulary (n = 86)

Agreement Language Skill	Strongly Agree (%)	Agree (%)	Neutral (%)	Disagree (%)	Strongly Disagree (%)
(a) Use correct sentence structures	23.3	61.6	15.1	0	0
(b) Use accurate grammar	10.4	53.5	30.3	1.1	0
(c) Use transitional elements	24.4	29.1	45.4	1.1	0
(d) Enlarge vocabulary	18.6	67.4	14.0	0	0

Extent of Using English Grammar, Structure, and Vocabulary

That they attempted to use correct sentence structures in doing the task was supported by a large majority (84.9%) of the students (see Table 3). Despite the fact that many agreed that they had used accurate grammar, there were some neutral responses (30.3%). This is possibly because most students from China were well versed in grammar, and as a result using accurate grammar was not something they had to put in much effort. Another reason may be that without accurate grammar in doing the task, students could guess the meaning of others' input through the content words and gestures used.

Table 3 shows 45.4% of the students were neutral about the use of transitional elements. A few students argued that there were too few transitional elements for them to consider and thus were ignored. However, I think otherwise. The fact that 45.4% showed neutral attitude towards the use of transitional elements, and that this aspect was subsequently ignored in the group discussion and in the final write-up of the story simply confirmed what I had suspected initially — students were weak in the use of transitional elements.

As regards vocabulary, the majority were agreeable that they had the chance to enlarge their word bank. This coincides with what I had observed and discussed in page 114 under the sub-heading of *Speaking and Listening*, that students had much to teach one another about new vocabulary.

Table 4. Extent of Using English Joyfully (n = 86)

Agreement / Language Skill	Strongly Agree (%)	Agree (%)	Neutral (%)	Disagree (%)	Strongly Disagree (%)
Enjoy using the English language	37.2	46.5	14.0	2.3	0

Extent of Using English Joyfully

Another of my intentions in using the oral strip story exercise was to provide an occasion for students to be themselves and to use English joyfully in a relaxed and pleasant atmosphere under minimal instructor's intervention. The creation of a low anxiety atmosphere would encourage performance to go up according to Curran (1972). If we subscribe to this, then the 83.7% of students (see Table 4) who said they enjoyed using the English language would be highly motivated to do the task and would have performed well in the use of the target language.

Generally, students thought the strip story task an interesting game for improving communication and language skills in English and called for similar games to be used in class. On the other hand, the main criticism was that the story was too easy and that each should have more sentences to memorise. Two students from one group protested strongly that the sentences in *The Thief and The Boy* were illogically arranged — their group came up with the story in Appendix C.1.

CONCLUSION

Given a sentence strip that was filled with words like *a thief*, *a mug*, or other interesting words, students would be eager to know what others had. Consequently, group members were motivated to exchange what they had, to discuss and argue the logic of the sentences, to look for grammar and transitional clues, and finally to figure out the whole story. In the process of completing the oral strip story assignment, the intermediate ESL Chinese students learned to work as a team — each in the group had a chance to speak, commanding other team members' attention. In so doing, each was encouraged to be articulate, using clear, audible, and correct pronunciation, sentence structures, and word usage to communicate effectively.

So, is the oral strip story a suitable activity for ESL/EFL students to experience real communication and language learning? The favourable comments, my observations, the student survey data, and the students' feedback suggest that students are positive about the worth of the oral strip story in helping them use and learn English. The oral strip story game has indeed provided a good chance for students to practise and improve the different language skills that they have learnt in class. Though speaking and listening are noticeable skills that students will use, the instructor can, however, steer the exercise to teaching other skill areas like pronunciation, grammar points and specific writing patterns.

As a total experience, one participant summed up the oral strip story as "A good game for students to participate in, because it makes students improve in almost every aspect of English language skills more or less. Since it is a more lively form than other exercises, students are more willing to participate in, and this game should be given out at least once."

REFERENCES

Auerbach, E. R. (1993). Reexamining English only in the ESL classroom. *TESOL Quarterly*, 27(1): 9–32.

Chomsky, N. (1969). Some observations in the teaching of language. *Pedagogic Reporter,* 21(2): 5–6, 13.

Curran, C.A. (1972). *Counselling-learning: A Whole-person Model for Education.* New York: Grune & Stratton

Gibson, E.M. (1978). The strip story: A catalyst for communication. In E.G. Joiner & P.B. Westphal (Eds.), *Developing Communication Skills: General Considerations & Specific Techniques* (pp. 130–35). Rowley, Massachussetts: Newbury House.

Harvey, John H.T. (1982). A communicational approach: Games II. In R.W. Blair (Ed.), *Innovative Approaches to Language Teaching* (pp. 204–213). Rowley, Massachussetts: Newbury House.

Johnson, F.C. (1973). *English as a Second Language: An Individualised Approach.* Singapore: Jacaranda Press.

Littlewood, W. (1981). *Communicative Language Teaching: An Introduction.* Cambridge, England: Cambridge University Press.

Stevick, E. (1982). *Teaching and Learning Languages.* Cambridge, England: University of Cambridge Press.

APPENDIX A. THE ORIGINAL VERSION OF *THE THIEF AND THE BOY*

A thief walked by a well one day and there he saw a Boy. The Boy started to cry and sob as though his heart would break.

"What's the matter with you?" said the Thief.

"Oh, my string broke and my silver mug fell down that well," blubbered the Boy between sobs.

"Isn't that just dandy!" said the Thief, and he tossed off his clothes and let himself down the well, thinking to steal the Boy's mug. He groped around and around, getting colder and wetter all the time, but he couldn't find the mug, because there wasn't any. So after a while he decided that the Boy had guessed he was a Thief and had sent him down the well to get him out of the way. Therefore, he gave up and climbed to the top. But when he got there both the Boy and the Thief's clothes were gone.

The Point → Never try to do to others what you don't want others to do to you.

APPENDIX B. STORIES WRITTEN BY STUDENTS

B.1 A Wooden Bowl

Long, long ago, there lived a boy with his family in a village. The boy had a grandpa and he loved his grandpa. Both the boy and the grandpa were supported by the boy's parent(sic).

Since the grandpa was getting older and older, he could not help the family anymore. The boy's parent began to get tired of hi. They forbid he old man to dine with the family.

One day, when the old man had his dinner, he dropped the bowl on the floor accidently and broke it. The couple was very angry. They gave the grandpa a wooden bowl in case of the old man dropping the bowl again.

Several days later, the couple saw there little son was carving on the wood.

"What are you doing?", the mother asked.

"Oh, I'm carving a wooden bowl," said the boy.

"What's it for?", asked the parent.

"I want to prepair(sic) a wooden bowl for you now. When you get old, you can also use it." The boy answered. Then the parents realised that they should be more kind to the old.

B.2 Careless People Get Carelessness

I had a classmate when I was in college, who seldom cared about other persons. When he was in the classroom, he turned on the radio loudly without thinking about others' complaints. When somebody was in trouble, he never offered his help. Even when other people donated for the people suffering disaster, he said ironically, "So silly! It's not your business!"

But with time went by, he paid much for his selfishness. He had few friends to play with and even nobody liked talking with him. Once he was really taught a lesson.

That was one week before the end of a semester. He didn't feel well for several days so that he missed several classes. Unfortunately, in one English class, the teacher informed us that because of some reason, the place of examination shifted to another classroom. He was not in the class, but nobody realised that. As a result, he was not informed so that he cannot find the place and he missed the examination!

Actually, we also feel very sad for him, but it's not our fault. If you never care about other people, how can you expect others willing to help you?

B.3 The Boy and The Monkey

One day a monkey stoled one watermelon from a field of a farm. He ran into a forest with the watermelon and wanted to eat it under a tall tree. There he saw a boy. The boy also saw the monkey and his watermelon. The monkey wanted to run away, but the boy said: "Hi monkey, why run away? You needn't be afraid of me, because you and me are the same kind of animal." The monkey felt confused, and said: "no, you are human being. Look, you have no tail, no thick hair everywhere like me. You walk mainly by foot, while I can walk by both hand and foot." The boy cried: "no, dear monkey, it is really true we are the same. Like, you can walk like me too. I can walk by both my hand and foot as you." The boy began to walk with his two hands and two feet. "And more," said the boy, "I can climb trees like you too." He climbed on one little tree beside the tall tree. After he climbed down, he asked the monkey, "Can you climb up this tree?" He pointed that tall tree. The monkey thought: "It's easy for us. He can only climb up that little tree!" Therefore he said to the boy: "Let me show you what's the difference between a monkey and a human being!" He left the watermelon on the ground and began to climb quickly. The tree was really tall and it took him five minutes to climb up to the top. The leaves were thick too. So he can't say the boy. He cried loudly: "Can you hear me? I have reached the top. It's just dandy for me to climb this tree. Unfortunately, he couldn't hear anything except the sound of the wind after a long time. So he climbed down the tree, and he saw the boy and his watermelon were all gone!

Point: Don't try to be clever than human being.

APPENDIX C. STUDENTS' VERSIONS OF *THE THIEF AND THE BOY*

C.1   A thief walked by a well, and there he saw a boy. They boy started to cry as though his heart would break. "What's the matter?" the thief asked. "Oh, my string broke, and my silver mug dropped in that well," blubbered the boy between sobs.

"Isn't that just dandy?" said the thief, and he tossed off his clothes, and let him go down the well, thinking to steal the boy's mug.

He groped around and around, getting colder and wetter, but he couldn't find the mug, because there wasn't any. Therefore, he gave up and climber to the top. When he climbed up, both the boy and the thief's clothes were gone. So, after a while, he decided that the boy knew he was a thief and sent him down the well and got him out of the way.

C.2 A thief walked by a well one day and there he saw a boy. "What's the matter with you" said the thief."My string broke and silver mug fell down to the well" Blubbered between the Bobs. The boy began to cry and sob as though his heart would break. "Isn't it a dandy". The thief tossed his clothes, let himself down the well, thinking of stealing the boy's mug.

He groped around, getting colder and wetter all the time, but he couldn't find any mug because there wasn't any. So he gave up and climbed to the top of the well. He decided that the Boy suggested he was a thief, and get don the well. When the boy came back there, the boy's and thief's clothes had gone.

APPENDIX D. SURVEY QUESTIONNAIRE ON THE ORAL STRIP STORY TASK

In completing the oral strip story, *The Thief and The Boy*, to what extent do you agree that you have used or learnt more about the following English language skills?

(Put a ✓ in the appropriate cell.)

Language skill \ Agreement	Strongly Agree	Agree	Neutral	Disagree	Strongly Disagree	Comments
(a) Speak clearly & audibly						
(b) Speak out boldly in a group						
(c) Use clear pronunciation						
(d) Listen actively & attentively						
(e) Think creatively						
(f) Write creatively						
(g) Use correct sentence structures						
(h) Use accurate grammar						
(i) Use transitional elements						
(j) Enlarge vocabulary						
(k) Enjoy using the English language						
(l) Others (please specify)						

Suggestions for Improvement:

CHAPTER 8

Using Children's Literature with Young Adult EFL Learners[1]

LAINA HO

WHY CHILDREN'S LITERATURE?

Teaching literature is beneficial in the language learning process because it provides valuable authentic material, cultural and language enrichment and personal involvement (Collie and Slater, 1987; Carter and Long 1987; Carter and Long, 1992). The rationale and effectiveness for using adult literature in the reading programme of adult EFL learners had been discussed and researched by language teachers such as Brumfit and Carter (1986) and Maley (2001) who advocated using it to enrich language learning and cultural knowledge, to gauge reading response, to teach literary criticism, and to raise the level of literary and language competence. Incorporating reading into EAP writing has been studied on a small scale by Hirvela (2001) who suggests that reading can become a more meaningful part in writing courses if students read and write in response to both literary and non-literary texts. However, he did not make a specific study on reading and writing in response to literary texts.

A variety of pedagogic activities in the language classroom can be provided by using literary works (Lazar, 1993; Carter and McRae, 1996; Ur, 1997; Maley, 2001) although it has been acknowledged that there may be problems such as length of the novel which poses a time constraint on classroom activities, the difficulty of vocabulary which impedes reading speed and reading comprehension, and the lack of cultural background knowledge which affects reading interest, all of

---

[1]Laina Ho acknowledges the permission of the English Teachers' Association of China — ROC to reprint this substantially revised version of her earlier work.

which can be particularly problematic for ESL and EFL learners (Lazar, 1990).

Is children's literature the answer to these problems? So far no study has been documented on teaching methodology using children's literature with adult EFL learners. Liaw (1998) mentioned the general instructional activities but not the response of EFL adult learners to children's literature. Taylor (2000) used folktales as an innovative way of teaching English to multilevel learners, but there has been no survey done on teaching children's literature to adult learners from the People's Republic of China. This study sets out to assess the role of children's literature in the EFL classroom and how it can be effectively used with EFL young adult learners from mainland China, whose English language education has basically concentrated on reading skills and vocabulary building (Dzau, 1990). Since there has been an increase of Chinese students going abroad to English-medium universities such as those in Singapore it is important that English language teachers are aware of the use of children's literature as potential material to vary teaching strategies and motivate language learning.

First of all, what is so special about children's literature other than that it is meant for children? Collie and Slater made the following observation:

> Children's literature is able to stimulate personal involvement, arousing learners' interest and provoking strong positive reactions from them, it is meaningful and enjoyable, and reading it has a lasting and beneficial effect upon learners' linguistic and cultural knowledge.
>
> (Collie & Slater, 1987: 6)

Other scholars who are more directly involved in children's literature and working with children show how it can offer a varied and wide range of literature from real life to imaginative topics. There are stories with well-developed characters, engaging plots and vivid themes, offering good sources of knowledge, particularly that on history and culture (folklore), sociological and psychological insights into realistic fiction, and a story framework for reading and writing as in exploring genres, oral responses, comprehending to composing, and enriching the arts and humanities, such as visual arts and drama, and encouraging the faculty of imagination (Bosma and DeVries Guth, 1995). Thirty years ago Isaac Bashevis Singer remarked, "children's literature has come to the fore, and that while adult literature, especially fiction, is deteriorating, the literature for children is gaining in quality and stature" (quoted in Townsend, 1973). I believe this is even truer today: witness the wide readership that has been generated from the recent furore over the *Harry Potter* books, which are read not only by children but also by adults.

THE ROLE OF CHILDREN'S LITERATURE IN THE EFL CLASSROOM

Advocates of children's literature testify to its usability and variety of activities in the classroom for children (Cullinan *et al.*, 1992). But how will adults respond to using children's literature to improve language skills? How can it be motivating for adult learners of English? How can it be used effectively in the language classroom in the same way as adult literature?

The students from the People's Republic of China were the first group of EFL learners at the Centre of English Language Communication to be given children's literature in their English lessons. Initially, I did not know how they would respond to children's literature but my rationale for introducing children's literature was based on the following observation. Firstly, they did not read much fiction in English, only Chinese translations of the English classics; secondly, their reading comprehension was poor, and therefore difficult vocabulary and linguistic style was a deterrent to reading; thirdly, though they were highly motivated students they should start with simple fiction progressing to difficult fiction for language acquisition. Most of all, like Ur (1997: 201) I simply wanted to introduce literature because I wanted them to enjoy reading and be motivated to acquire language skills on their own.

The research participants were young PRC adult learners, averaging 18 years who come from the Northeastern, Central, Western and Southeastern parts of China. I introduced children's literature to my students starting with short stories for my classroom language lessons. There were three groups of students, 20 in each, a third of which were females. I taught each group every year in the second semester from 1996–99.

HOW CHILDREN'S LITERATURE IS USED IN THE EFL CLASSROOM

At first I was not certain how I would use children's books but when I found that they were reading only academic texts and non-fiction outside the classroom I decided that at this stage in their language learning they could start by improving vocabulary (Dole *et al.*, 1995). Adult literature, however, was too difficult because, they informed me, "there are too many difficult words, the style of writing is too complex and the sentences are all so long". I therefore chose a short story from Geraldine McCaughrean's award-winning novel, *A Pack of Lies*, a collection of short stories. This story is called *The Plate: a question of values*, a re-telling of the *Willow Pattern Plate*. I thought it should be interesting and familiar to my students as it is set in China. I chose this story because I wanted to introduce English fiction that was within the reading ability of my students but at the same time would be challenging in terms of linguistic and literary qualities. I read aloud the story to them first and then gave individual reading practice. What I found interesting was that using children's literature in the EFL classroom can teach several important aspects of the language as the following sections will report.

Pronunciation Practice

When my students read aloud *The Plate: a question of values*, I found that they could not do this well. Consider this paragraph:

> The *orange blossom* was tearful with *rain. The willow tree* by the *lake* slumped with *rounded* shoulders. The *lake glimmered through the reeds like* teardrops on the lashes of a *great* sad eye. Wa Fan looked for a *long* time at the little bridge hunched over the *lake.*
>
> (*A Pack of Lies*, p.46)

The italicised words are difficult for my students because they contain the difficult consonants, /r/, /l/ and /θ/ in successive words. Particularly difficult are these consonants at the beginning of words. Thus *the lake glimmered through the reeds like teardrops on the lashes of a great sad eye* when read by my students sounded like, *the lake gimmered though the leeds nike teardrops on the lashes of a geat sad eye.* The students from Central China tended to substitute /l/ for /n/ and vice versa, such as *like* pronounced as *nike.* In isolation, these words pose no difficulty for my students but in this prose, they tend to drop the /l/ or /θ/ when read in a continuous paragraph, and may sound unintelligible to anyone not familiar with the difficulty that Chinese speakers have with these consonants.

In spite of the difficulty my students found children's literature more interesting than the drills in prescribed pronunciation textbooks because of the challenge it poses for dramatised reading. They had to learn to read with the correct intonation, pitch, stress, diction and enunciation. What I hoped to do here was to make the students become aware of the challenge that children's literature has to offer in terms of reading aloud and pronunciation practice; other than prose children's literature like rhymes and poems offer a challenge in pronunciation practice, for instance, nursery rhymes like *Row, Row, Row Your Boat* and Dr Seuss' *Oh the Thinks You Can Think!* Granted that fiction texts require more expressive reading and are therefore particularly difficult for EFL learners, children's literature can prove a challenge even to advanced learners of English, especially those who relish challenge. But whether difficult or easy, EFL learners can become more aware of the potential of children's literature in developing oral and reading skills. Furthermore, after reading a story like *The Plate: a question of values,* my Chinese students have become more aware of literary style. This leads us to the next interesting lesson with my students.

Teaching Literary Styles

Assuming that literary style could be taught easily since these are intelligent students well versed in the Chinese classics and linguistically and literarily competent in their native literature with the ability to distinguish between quality and non-quality writing, I taught them the literariness of narration in *The Plate: a question of values.* I drew their attention to some phrases explaining that these are literary techniques used by English authors and poets: From the same paragraph I pointed out some examples of similes, metaphors, personification, alliterations, rhyme and rhythm.

like teardrops on the lashes of a great sad eye — simile
slumped with rounded shoulders — personification
tearful with rain — metaphor
The lake glimmered through the reed like — alliteration

The whole paragraph, when read aloud, has a melancholic rhythm that reflects the poignancy of the narration.

Another example of prose set my student thinking about similar literary devices used in Chinese literature:

In old China, during the Ch'ing dynasty and in the days of the Manchu Emperor Ch'ien Lung, a daughter's words were worth less than dead leaves blowing down a street. But the birds of sadness pecked at her heart.

(The Plate: a question of values, p.45)

And further down, in another paragraph using parallel structure:

For in old China, during the Ch'ng dynasty and in the days of the Manchu Emperor Ch'ien Lung, the words of an apprentice were worth less than the ants in a spadeful of earth. But inwardly the dogs of sadness chewed on his heart.

(The Plate: a question of values, p.46)

My students gleefully pointed out to me that they have similar Chinese expressions — "my heart pierced by a thousand arrows" or "a million pins sticking into my heart". It was as though they had suddenly become enlightened to the fact that English literature is very much like Chinese literature, and therefore, they could be more discriminating and selective when choosing English fiction to read.

My students' enthusiasm for this story made me think that perhaps since it was a familiar story they could therefore appreciate it because of cultural identification and empathy. So I decided to choose another story, this time set in India, from *A Pack of Lies.* I asked them if they could point out the literary devices for me, using this paragraph from *The Writing Box: a story of a liar:*

India sweltered under a sky the colour of bruises. The air was thick with flies. A rain of mosquitoes and blowflies beat into her

> face, and the light hurt her eyes. At night, the dark leaned on her
> as if exhausted by the heat, and the undergrowth hummed with
> the promise of huge, grotesque insects.
>
> *(The Writing Box: a story of a liar,* p.35)

My students had a bit of difficulty with identifying the figurative
language especially the metaphors, but they managed to identify the
simile in, "as if exhausted by the heat". They could identify the others
but could not name the literary techniques. However, since this was
not a literature test, it was not important that they could not name
these. While their comments on the figurative language were not
competent enough their response showed that they could appreciate
quality writing and had become more aware of literary works in
fiction. This would help them in selecting titles, both adult and
children's, they wished to read for language acquisition. In addition
to learning literary styles and techniques, my students found that
children's literature is not easy reading as they had thought at first.
This is because of the vocabulary, for example, *sweltered, bruises,
grotesque, cuffed, pagodas, clattered, gnawing,* and so on from *The
Plate* and *The Writing Box.*

On the whole, their comments about the two stories they had read
so far, were positive — "the language sounds very nice and interesting;
it is very well written, you know this because when you read it the
words are so descriptive and nice sounding". They had learned quickly
to appreciate the richness of literary styles and language of children's
books, where good writers "delight in their creative but precise use
of words, words which appeal directly to the emotions and the
imagination" (Nicoll, 1993: 370).

To give them another chance to show off their newfound knowledge
of literary style I decided to give them a lesson on literary criticism.
It would also encourage them to openly express individual opinions,
an activity I found lacking among Chinese students because they were
not used to such open discussions. A lesson on literary criticism would
also teach critical thinking, again an activity that seems stifled among
Chinese students. This is not to say that my students could not think
critically; they could, but they needed a lot of encouragement to speak
up, even when their contributions were not relevant.

Teaching Literary Criticism/Reading Response

As I was in a hurry to complete the syllabus for this intensive English course I decided to use the same story, *The Plate: a question of values* again. This is a familiar Chinese folk tale about two young lovers — a poor potter and the daughter of a wealthy merchant — who elope in the face of parental objection and manage to board a foreign ship out of China. Though it was familiar and not so "interesting" in plot, the students offered some penetrating insight on the unusual ending. While some of the students (mostly females) preferred a tragic ending with lots of pathos (as in most Chinese love stories), the others were rather thrilled with the story ending. The original story of *The Willow Pattern Plate* had the lovers falling off a bridge and drowning together but the gods smiled on them, turning them into bluebirds so that they could live happily ever after.

In McCaughrean's story, the lovers have a chance to find a new life in a foreign land by using the willow pattern plate as their ticket to freedom when they board a Portuguese ship. My students admired the unconventional behaviour of the lovers who show disobedience and unfilialness, selfishness and rebelliousness by running away. They admired the guts and ingenuity of the young lovers. Besides, this story was set in the Qing (Manchu) dynasty, and since China was opening to the West, young Chinese should shake off the shackles of Imperial China and its old feudal ways and customs and look to the New World for inspiration and modernisation. Thus, one of them said, "Maybe you will question the possibility of the two lovers' success in running away, but I think it doesn't matter; it just indicates that people's struggles against the restrictions can succeed one day." In short, this story symbolises for my Chinese students the spirit of freedom under repression and authoritarianism. Taken in today's political context, they seem to imply that their present government seems repressive and old-fashioned. Coming from a country with centuries of historical turmoil, these students were able to read more into a simple love story like *The Plate: a question of values*, taking the flight for freedom as a symbolism for the fight for individual rights and democracy, a view that I had never considered before, having read it as a children's story with the typical happy ending (Ho, 2000: 264). This exercise has shown me that the reading response of my Chinese students can be different from readers unfamiliar with the culture and values depicted in the story. Because they are older, they are able to successfully evaluate the story at the critical and aesthetic levels (Sebesta *et al.*, 1995).

Similarly, their response to *The Writing Box: the story of a liar* shows me that they had more perceptiveness than I. This is a story of a Victorian girl whose parents left her in a boarding school in England when they were assigned to serve in the civil service of British India. Grace is a terrible liar and bully, a lazy pupil trying desperately to get away to India because she thinks England is boring. Once there she finds India a trying place and bullies her maid, implicates her in a theft and out of spite, because her ruse did not work, cuts off her maid's long black hair. For this Grace is bitten by a poisonous snake planted in her writing box by her maid's fiancé, and dies.

The moral of the story is that children should not lie, but the moral of the story for my Chinese students is that revenge is justified. They read this story as an "empire strikes back" kind of morality, that the British colonial masters deserve their punishment for lording it over the natives. They may consciously or unconsciously have some prejudice against Westerners who humiliated the Qing rules in the 19th century but they, who love Chinese martial arts stories where the dashing knight-errant risks life and death to save the less fortunate and the downtrodden and who will kill without a blink of the eye, to avenge the wrongs, would certainly feel that justice has been meted in this story. Thus they felt no tinge of pity or regret that though Grace is only a child, her behaviour being the result of parental neglect, she nevertheless deserves her fate (Ho, 2000: 265).

The third short story from *A Pack of Lies* is *The Clock: a story of superstition*, set in Ireland. This is a story of a very superstitious but wealthy Irishman who rears Derby-winning racehorses, and who brings about his own miserable end because he foolishly believes in fortune-telling. My students' response was not as enthusiastic as for the other two stories because they said, "it's like all those Chinese stories we read before about some foolish peasant, and it is not interesting or even funny. We can't believe that Westerners are so superstitious." Their rather bland response shows their impatience with a familiar theme, a result, I suspect, of frequent indoctrination against the old ways. This does not mean they disliked the story. They appreciated the figurative language, some of which raised a chuckle or two as in, "The trees shook their branches at him menacingly, and roof slates lay in wait, ready to throw themselves at his head and brain him" (*A Pack of Lies*, p.20). Also, they were intrigued by the references to Irish culture: leprechauns and witches, Sunday mass (Christian ritual in juxtaposition to superstitious practices) and gypsy, all of which generated a special lesson and discussion because of their keenness to learn.

These lessons show that PRC learners can make sufficient and satisfactory critical comments and write about these criticisms in their essays. But to be able to do this the literary works must be simple for their reading comprehension and require little cultural background (none of the PRC students knew much about India except that it was formerly ruled by the British) and stories must have good characterisation, themes, simple and interesting plots and a propelling narrative style.

Creative Writing Through Dramatisation

As an extension of this exercise that the students enjoyed, I gave them another short story from *One Thousand and One Arabian Nights* to see if they could turn this story into a creative writing exercise. I chose *The Everlasting Shoes*, one of the stories in the collection. This is a different writing skill compared to their everyday writing assignments but the students proved, to my surprise, that they could be just as imaginative and creative as the author. Naturally, I gave them one or two examples of how to write drama scripts but then these Chinese students are familiar with Chinese opera and Chinese theatrical performances and could put their drama writing skills in this story. *The Everlasting Shoes* is a very funny story about a miserable miser of Cairo who loses all his fortune because of his despicable shoes. My students enjoyed the story even though it contains a lot of difficult vocabulary but I explained unfamiliar words and phrases including any unfamiliar Arabian culture to them. The students worked on the scripts in groups of four and turned the story into a bloodthirsty, mud-slinging, slapstick comedy. They showed they could be as colourful in their language as the author, transferring some of the most expressive phrases in their Chinese language to English. For example:

> Abu Kassim throws his smelly shoes into the miller's pool, stopping the mill from turning. The miller discovers the source of the problem.

Miller: What an awful smell, it must be Kassim's shoes. The damned dog! He must pay for this!

Kassim is on his way home, whistling. He has a grin, as wide as a watermelon slice.

Kassim: Today it's another beginning of my life!

The miller catches up with Kassim and seizes him by the scuff of his neck.

Kassim: Oi, what are you doing?

Miller: You ask me? You should know! Look at this pair of shoes carefully. Even a worm can recognise it's yours!

Kassim: Yes, they used to be but I have thrown them away. How did you get them?

Miller: You're as stupid as a pig! The shoes floated down into my mill and made a mess of my mill. You come with me! Let the police deal with this.

Although this script is not perfect, for these students from China it was a good effort as it shows that they have their own brand of Chinese humour which makes them so appreciative of *The Everlasting Shoes*. It is their lack of English vocabulary and speech discourse that makes the dialogue sound stilted, but it was a rich and rewarding language experience. What makes *The Everlasting Shoes* so appealing to my students is that it has an international appeal — the plot is easy to follow, the characterisation identifiable (stinginess is not a vice of any particular race) and though the setting is foreign, it does not detract. It was also rather astounding to see these young adults throwing off their inhibitions and shyness when they acted the parts of the characters from their scripts, compared to the first time I met them when some could hardly utter an intelligible sentence in English. I do not think the same students could have done so well if I had given them an adult play say, by Oscar Wilde. Introducing adult plays can come later but first they need the confidence by starting with something simple.

LIMITATIONS

Though it can be assumed that highly motivated EFL learners from the People's Republic of China will read anything, even children's picture books, for language learning, children's literature also has limitations. Basically, characterisation is a stumbling block. It offers little empathy for adult readers. Therefore, we cannot expect young adult EFL learners to be continually given children's stories for assignments or classroom activities. Nor can we expect them to show a continuing interest in reading for language acquisition when the protagonists are children. There is a possibility that young adults like my students would prefer adolescent literature, but this will merit another study on the use of adolescent literature with EFL learners. An assessment of the readability of teenage fiction from reader response of ESL adolescent readers shows that in teenage fiction, language which is seemingly simpler but with an I-narration type of conversational monologue spiced up with unabashed teenage humour can be appealing in terms of reading interest (Ho, 1992). Consider a teenage novel like Ursula Le Guin's *A very long way from anywhere else* with an opening paragraph like this, which many of the ESL Singapore readers surveyed in a readability study (Ho, 2000) found appealing:

> If you like a story about how I won my basketball colours and achieved fame, love, and fortune, don't read this. I don't know what I achieved in the six months I'm going to tell about. I achieved something, all right, but I think it may take me the rest of my life to find out what.
>
> (*A very long way from anywhere else*, p.1)

It can be predicted that adolescent fiction, mostly realistic, about teenage angst or rite of passage, may be more appealing than children's literature for young adult EFL readers (Thomson, 1987). Teenage novels have recently moved away from the usual theme of "rite of passage" in the popular "problem novels" from the United States. Instead young adult novels nowadays offer more in terms of cultural identity for non-native English readers, for example, books like Alan Baillie's *The China Coin* is about a Eurasian girl's visit to her Chinese ancestral village, with the Tiananmen incident as the catalyst to the ending. This novel and other multi-cultural, multi-racial novels published as teenage novels can be studied in the EFL classroom without presenting the problem of identity alienation for adult learners.

However, this is not to say that children's literature cannot be used with adult learners of English. Certainly the stories which were used in this study have adult characterisation particularly in folk tales, legends and mythology, and were successful with my students. But there are also good short stories with adult protagonists in contemporary settings such as the collection of short stories in *A Pack of Lies*. Children's science fiction should pose no difficulty for my students who may also find fantasy or supernatural tales interesting. A few examples of titles which may work with adult learners of English based on my knowledge and observation of PRC students are: Robert O'Brien's *Mrs. Frisby and the Rats of NIMH,* Diana Wynne Jones' *Howl's Moving Castle,* Roald Dahl's *The Wonderful World of Henry Sugar,* Roger Lancelyn Green's *King Arthur and His Knights of the Round Table,* J.R.R.Tolkien's *The Hobbit,* John Christopher's *The Prince in Waiting,* Mary Norton's *The Borrowers Avenged* and Meindert Dejong's *The House of Sixty Fathers.* The list is not exhaustive but generally speaking, science fiction, mythology/ legends and fantasy genres may be more successful in arousing reading interest among adult readers as they will not be able to identify with the child protagonist in realistic fiction. Historical fiction is not suitable, especially Western history, as it is unfamiliar for EFL readers from East Asia.

As this study was confined to short stories, more study will be needed to find how EFL adult learners will respond to other genres or to a complete children's novel and even children's poems, especially if chosen for pronunciation practice. Further investigation should certainly include the study of the use of adolescent literature, especially the modern teenage novel which can provide a sense of empathy and identity for the young adult readers.

CONCLUSION

The rationale for using children's literature in the EFL classroom is based on two factors. The first is that in general, EFL learners are linguistically not ready for adult literature, and second, children's literature can be comparable to adult literature in offering a variety of pedagogic activities (Bosma and DeVries Guth, 1995; Cullinan 1992), teaching practice (Waterland, 1990) as well as in other aspects of learning skills such as, "promoting high level discussion and critical thinking — needs that the adult literacy student shares" (Handel and Goldsmith, 1989: 25). The criteria by which children's literature can appeal to adult learners include the challenge it offers for developing oral skills in pronunciation and reading practice, vocabulary building, appreciation of English literary styles, practice in literary criticism and, developing creative writing in the dramatisation of stories. Moreover, children's fiction texts with illustrations to aid comprehension is an advantage (Appelt, 1985). Indeed, children's picture books like *One Thousand and One Arabian Nights*, with visually stunning illustrations can be stimulating language learning even for EFL advanced students because picture books have "aesthetic value" and "employ sophisticated narrative techniques" (Benton and Fox, 1985: 74). Children's picture books also offer more pronunciation features such as rhyming words, metre, varieties of pitch, intonation, stress patterns, diction, demanding a more dramatised reading. The simplicity of the storyline, plots, narrative styles, themes, setting and the shorter length of children's literature may be effective for TOEFL teachers working within a time constraint and with EFL learners whose linguistic level is low.

Basically, having had a 'taste' of children's literature, EFL learners like my Chinese students have come to realise that it is compatible and comparable to adult literature, and that it can be read not solely for academic purpose but also for pleasure. Reading children's literature proved to be an enjoyable and stimulating experience for my students. Although this observation applies to Chinese EFL learners, other EFL learners should find children's literature interesting for language learning.

The potential of children's literature in EFL teaching is considerable as East Asian countries are gearing up to increase awareness of the importance and universal usage of the English language. The reading interest shown by the students in this study indicates that children's literature can be introduced in the reading programme of EFL classroom as a vital initial step towards improving literacy. Naturally, children's literature is not the solution to problems on language teaching in the EFL classroom and it should not be offered as a constant dosage to ward off tedium from ESP academic materials, but rather as and when necessary. It should be used where appropriate such as with EFL learners in developing countries where English is a foreign language. Children's literature can open up a lot of avenues for language learning activities, reading programmes, literature studies, and creative workshops such as drama and art and craft, not just for children but also for adult learners of English.

REFERENCES

Appelt, J.E. (1985). Not just for little kids: The picture book in ESL classes. *TESL Canada Journal,* 2: 67–78.

Brumfit, C.J. & Carter R.A. (Eds.) (1986). *Literature and Language Teaching.* Oxford: Oxford University Press.

Benton, M. & Fox, G. (1985). *Teaching Literature 9–14.* Oxford: Oxford University Press.

Bosma, B. & DeVries Guth, N. (Eds.) (1995). *Children's Literature in an Integrated Curriculum.* New York: Teachers College Press.

Carter, R. & Long, M.N. (1987). *The Web of Words: Exploring Literature Through Language.* Cambridge: Cambridge University Press.

_____ (1992). *Teaching Literature.* Essex: Longman.

Carter, R. & McRae, J. (Eds.) (1996). *Language, Literature and the Learner: Creative Classroom Practice.* London: Longman.

Collie, J. & Slater, S. (1987). *Literature in the Language Classroom.* Cambridge: Cambridge University Press.

Cullinan, B. (Ed.) (1992). *Invitation to Read: More Children's Literature in the Reading Program.* Newark: International Reading Association.

Dole, J. *et al.* (1995). Teaching vocabulary within the context of literature. *Journal of Adolescent and Adult Literacy,* 38(6): 452–60.

Dzau, Y.F. (1990). How English is taught in tertiary educational institutions. In Y.F. Dzau (Ed.), *English in China* (pp. 41–58). Hong Kong: API Press.

Handel, R. & Goldsmith, E. (1989). Children's literature and adult literacy: Empowerment through intergenerational learning. *Lifelong Learning: An Omnibus of Practice and Research,* 12(6): 24–27.

Hirvela, A. (2001). Incorporating reading into EAP writing courses. In J. Flowerdew & M. Peacock (Eds.), *Research Perspectives on English for Academic Purposes* (pp. 330–46). Cambridge: Cambridge University Press.

Ho, L. (2000). Children's literature in adult education. *Children's Literature in Education,* 31(4): 259–72.

_____ (2000). Readability of American and British teens fiction — a reader response assessment. *Working Papers* 7: 20–37. Singapore: Centre for English Language Communication, National University of Singapore.

_____ (1992). American teens books easier than British ones. *Journal of Reading,* 35(4): 324–27.

Lazar, G. (1990). Using novels in the language-learning classroom. *ELT Journal,* 44: 204–214.

_____ (1993). *Literature and Language Teaching.* Cambridge: Cambridge University Press.

Liaw, Meei-Ling (1998). American Children's Literature: An Alternative Choice for EFL Instruction. *Proceedings from the Seventh International Symposium on English Teaching.* Taipei, pp. 683–93.

Maley, A. (2001). Literature in the language classroom. In Ronald Carter and David Nunan (Eds.), *The Cambridge Guide to Teaching English to Speakers of Other Languages* (pp. 180–85). Cambridge: Cambridge University Press.

Nicoll, V. (1993). Language and Literature: The Classroom Experience. In Maurice Saxby and Gordon Winch (Eds.), *Give The Wings: The Experience of Children's Literature* (pp. 369–404). Sydney: Macmillan.

Sebesta, S. *et al.* (1995). A hierarchy to assess reader response. *Journal of Adolescent and Adult Literacy,* 38(6): 444–50.

Taylor, E.K. (2000). *Using Folktales.* Cambridge: Cambridge University Press.

Thomson, J. (1987). *Understanding Teenagers' Reading: Reading Processes and the Teaching of Literature.* Melbourne: Methuen.

Townsend, J.R. (1973). The Present State of English Children's Literature. *Literature for Children Unit 2* (pp. 21–27). Milton Keynes: Open University.

Ur, P. (1997). *A Course in Language Teaching.* Cambridge: Cambridge University Press.

Waterland, L. (1990). *Apprenticeship in Action: Teachers Write About Read With Me.* Exeter: Thimble Press.

CHILDREN'S BOOKS CITED

Baillie, A. (1990). *The China Coin.* Harmondsworth: Puffin.

Christopher, John (1977). *The Prince in Waiting.* London: Hamish Hamilton.

Dahl, Roald (1977). *The Wonderful World of Henry Sugar.* Harmondsworth: Puffin.

DeJong, Meindert. (1966). *The House of Sixty Fathers.* Harmondsworth: Puffin.

Dr Seus (1984). *Oh The Thinks You Can Think.* London: Collins.

Lancelyn Green, Roger (1984). *King Arthur and His Knights of the Round Table.* Harmondsworth: Puffin.

Le Guin, Ursula (1988). *A Very Long Way From Anywhere Else.* Harmondsworth: Puffin.

McCaughrean, G. (1985). *One Thousand and One Arabian Nights.* Oxford: Oxford University Press.

_____ (1988). *A Pack of Lies.* Oxford: Oxford University Press.

Norton, Mary (1982). *The Borrowers Avenged.* Harmondsworth: Puffin.

O'Brien, Robert (1982). *Mrs. Frisby and the Rats of NIMH.* Harmondsworth: Puffin.

Tolkien, J.R.R. (1987). *The Hobbit.* London: Allen and Unwin.

Wynne Jones, Diana (1992). *Howl's Moving Castle.* London: Methuen.

CHAPTER 9

Pronunciation Problems of PRC Students

LAINA HO

INTRODUCTION

The Centre for English Language Communication has been teaching the SM3 students since 1992. One of the main problems with these PRC students is their speaking skills. At the beginning many students could hardly utter an intelligible sentence in English because of their poor pronunciation; sometimes it was their lack of fluency as well as grammatical accuracy. More often it was poor pronunciation that hindered communication between them and non-PRC people. While non-PRC teachers at CELC are usually able to understand their PRC students' spoken English fairly accurately, they are still unable to comprehend their students fully because this "unintelligibility"[1] quite often arises from the interference of students' mother tongue affecting the pronunciation. This poor pronunciation could also be the result of insufficient practice in pronunciation drills in English learning classroom in China, where the main emphasis was reading comprehension and vocabulary building (Feng, 1999 and 2000).

Most research shows that there is learner's native language interference in the target language leading to difficulty in pronunciation (Wu, 1993; Flege, 1980). Other research observes that learners utter English phonemes by searching the corresponding sound in their native language first, and then substituting the target sound with it (Hockett, 1972; Lado, 1957). Li (1998) explored the common errors made in

---

[1]"Intelligibility" defined as "the more words a listener is able to identify accurately when said by a particular speaker, the more intelligible that speaker is" (Kenworthy, 1998: 13).

pronunciation of English consonants used in American English by Chinese learners in Taiwan and attributed these errors to substitution, deletion and insertion problems because there are no corresponding English consonant sounds in Mandarin. Huang (1998) observed that poor listening skills of Taiwanese English learners contributed quite considerably to poor pronunciation while Chan and Li (2000) explained why pronunciation problems occur among Cantonese speakers learning English in Hong Kong and offered some insightful understanding of their pronunciation difficulty based on their observation of the fundamental differences between the phoneme inventories of English and Cantonese as well as the characteristics and distribution of the phonemes. Kelly identified the main phoneme difficulties of Chinese learners besides other speakers of English to help EFL teachers teach pronunciation (Kelly, 2000:144–46).

This study, on the other hand, sets out to identify the specific pronunciation problems, vowels as well as consonants, of Chinese learners from certain regions of China because this is a less studied area. Naturally, this will not be a complete study as a substantial knowledge of the varieties of Chinese dialects spoken in the different regions of China is necessary in order to understand the interference or substitution of the native language on English phonetic sounds. It is, however, possible to contrast the sounds in the common Chinese dialects found in Malaysia and Singapore, such as Yue (Guangzhou)[2], Min (Fujian, Chaozhou), Hakka (Southern Jiangxi, Guangxi, Northern Guangzhou) (Ramsey, 1987:87–115) and the interference on English sounds but the majority of the PRC pre-matriculation students in this sample group were not from the Southern regions of China. Except for a small number from the Guangzhou province, the rest were from the Northern, Western and Central regions of China where a variety of Mandarin Chinese is spoken (Ting, 1991:186–236). However, working in Singapore, notwithstanding the lack of substantial Chinese dialectical knowledge, it is feasible to identify and understand to some extent, though not all, the causes of some common pronunciation problems that affect the intelligibility of PRC students who have been studying in CELC since 1996. These include the pre-matriculated students as well as the postgraduate students from China.

---

[2]These provinces (in parenthesis) are the most common regions from which the Malaysian and Singapore overseas Chinese originated.

As such, this study is concerned with presenting the most important features of the pronunciation problems of our Chinese learners at CELC as observed by our teachers. It aims to identify those problems which are important for a "comfortable" intelligibility (Kenworthy, 1998:3) rather than a native-like pronunciation (Harmer, 2001:184; Abercombie, 1991:93). It will also recommend teaching methodology that would consider the socio-cultural factors of PRC students in accordance with the generally accepted "uniquely sensitive nature of pronunciation teaching in comparison with other skills such as mastering grammar and vocabulary" (Seidlhofer, 2001:58). These teaching strategies could be useful and motivating, both to learners and teachers from this Centre and elsewhere. It is hoped that EFL teachers would become more aware of the major pronunciation problems of PRC students, understand the causes of these problems and help their students improve their pronunciation.

This paper has two parts: the first identifies the most common pronunciation difficulties peculiar to students from different regions of China and discusses possible reasons for them, taking into consideration the interference of L1 on L2; the second part recommends tips for EFL teachers to make teaching pronunciation interesting and effective for EFL adult Chinese learners.

RESEARCH SET-UP

Participants

Number of students: 39
Female students: 12
Male students: 27
20 students were from the 1996 group
19 students were from 1998 group

Number of students from:
Central China (Hubei, Henan, Sichuan): 16
Northeastern China (Beijing, Shandong): 6
Central East China (Suzhou, Hangzhou): 5
Southeastern China (Guangzhou, Shenzhen): 12

Procedure

Two videotaped oral presentations of the 39 PRC students who took the Intensive English course in 1996 and 1998, were transcribed. The oral presentations were individual tasks and each student spoke on general topics relevant to the China scene, such as "A Chinese Festival, My Hometown, Environmental Problems, High School Education in China", and so on. To verify the findings a set of questionnaires was given to 20 tutors from CELC who have taught either the PRC Intensive English Course or the Postgraduate Intermediate English Course for students from the PRC.

FINDINGS

Generally, the students from Central China such as Hubei, Henan and Shandong have the worst pronunciation problems in terms of intelligibility while those from the coastal cities such as Suzhou, Guangzhou and Beijing have the least, and are more fluent as they may have more access to English programmes on radio and television.

The following results were transcribed from two videotaped presentations of the PRC students' short talk lasting about 10 minutes for each speaker (see Appendix A).

Consonants

Rank in descending order starting with the most difficult:

/r/ and /l/	Really, truly, row, Larry, rely, lorry, rail, literary, regal
/r/	Crew, grow, fright, rather, grass, rot, row, frog
/l/	Boil, spoil, furl, pull, all, full, call, gall, goal, tail
/θ/	Thin, three, thigh, truth, thug, breathe, seethe, bath
/ŋ/	Sing, clung, stung, ring, thing, wing, sling, gong
/ʃ/	Shop, she, shall, show, short, shine, she'll, short, sheet
/tʃ/	Rich, fetch, cheer, much

Consonants in pairs

Rank in descending order starting with the most difficult:

/k/ and /g/   Lack–lag, rick–rig, flock–flog, clue–glue, crumble–grumble
/f/ and /v/   Fine–vine, few–view, a life–alive, rifle–rival, leaf–leave
/t/ and /d/   Tin–din, ton–done, latter–ladder, writer–rider
/p/ and /b/   Pet–bet, park–bark, a brooch–approach, pride–bride, wrap it–rabbit

The following results are the responses of CELC teachers who have taught PRC students.

Consonants

Rank in descending order starting with the most difficult:

/θ/   Thin, thigh, truth, breathe, bath
/r/ and /r/ & /l/   Crew, fright, rather, rot, really, lorry, rely, literary
/l/   Soil, furl, load, let, tail, all
/ŋ/   Sing, clung, thing, sling
/ʃ/   Shop, she, show, short, sheet
/tʃ/   Rich, fetch, cheer, much

Consonants in pairs

Rank in descending order starting with the most difficult:

/k/ and /g/   Lack–lag, rick–rig, flock–flog, clue–glue
/f/ and /v/   Fine–vine, few–view, a life–alive, rifle–rival
/t/ and /d/   Tin–din, ton–done, latter–ladder, writer–rider
/p/ and /b/   Pet–bet, park–bark, a brooch–approach, pride–bride

Most PRC students have difficulty with /r/ and /l/ especially students from Southern China. Although 69.2% of CELC teachers noted that /θ/ is the most difficult from their teaching experience, 43.3% of CELC teachers ranked /r/ and /l/ in isolation as well as /r/ and /l/ occurring in polysyllabic words, as the second most difficult. It is particularly problematic in polysyllabic words containing both /r/ and /l/ where words are mispronounced. A word like *generally* is reduced to a two-syllabic word — *gen-li* and sometimes into three-syllabic — *genrali*, depending on the pace of speech. Where /r/ and /l/ occur in two-syllabic words many Chinese students will drop the /l/. For example, *world* becomes *word*, *curl* becomes *cur*, *results* becomes *resuts*. 42% of CELC teachers agree strongly with this observation. Northern Chinese students can produce /r/ fairly accurately when it appears in one-syllabic words. This is because in the Beijing Chinese accent, an /r/ sound, almost similar to the English /r/ (except that the tip of the tongue does not roll back as much as the English /r/) is often tagged on the end of a word such as "wan" ("play" in Chinese) which is pronounced as "wan-r". In Chinese text this symbol [ʃㄦ] is tagged on to the Chinese character as an indication that the word must be read with a "r" sound. The Beijing dialect has a strong tendency to use final retroflex /r/ for words that have final *n* historically, for example, in words like *biar* from *bian* (side), *idiar* from *yi dian* (a little) and *menr* from *men* (door) (Barale, 1982: 155). This /r/ sound is a mark of elegant Beijing pronunciation as Ramsey explained,

> This particular pronunciation, which strongly recalls the /r/ of the American Midwest, is very much admired. The great majority of Chinese living outside of the capital itself are unable to pronounce this sound correctly when they speak Putonghua, (Mandarin Chinese) and most do not even try to imitate it.
>
> (Ramsey, 1987: 43)

It is not surprising that the Northern Chinese students have less difficulty with one-syllabic or two-syllabic words ending with /r/ and /l/ as in *girl, furl, curl, hurl*. This observation is borne out by some CELC teachers who said that Northern Chinese are seemingly used to the /r/ in their own native dialects. But inadvertently the tendency to roll out the /r/ sounds may result in incorrect pronunciation. The Beijing students, for example, because of their familiarity with the /r/ sound, sometimes put in extra /r/ sound in most words containing either /r/ or /l/. For instance, *everyone* becomes *everryone, usually* becomes *urrually*. This habit is noted by 50% of CELC teachers.

On the whole, most Chinese students have a problem with words containing /r/ and /l/ whether in two-syllabic or polysyllabic words whereas they have less difficulty in pronouncing monosyllabic words containing either /r/ or /l/. However, there may be exceptions to this observation such as the students from Henan and Hubei (see **Specific Pronunciation Problems**). The /l/ at the beginning of monosyllabic word is fairly easy as in Putonghua there is a "le" sound, so transferring this sound to /l/ is not very difficult. /l/ at the end of words such as *tail, fail, mall, nail, tell,* are less accurate for some students who tend to produce the /r/ sound instead because they cannot stop rolling back their tongue. CELC teachers (57%) agree strongly with this observation. /r/, on the other hand, is more difficult, particularly at the beginning of words, for example, *roar, run, rob, ring, read.* /r/ at the end of words is easier as in *boar, oar, hair.* Again, it seems that Chinese students, other than those from Northern China, have become used to the [ɟ L] tagged at certain Chinese characters in reading texts in schools. This may explain why many Chinese learners have not much difficulty in pronouncing words ending with /r/.

The second most difficult sound for most Chinese learners is the fricative /θ/ either at the beginning or end of words. CELC teachers consider this sound to be the most difficult for their PRC students because there is no such sound in Mandarin (Li, 1998: 640; Kenworthy, 1998:128), and perhaps because many students are shy of putting the tip of their tongue between the teeth to produce the soundless but aired /θ/. They tend to substitute the sound /θ/ for /s/. Thus *thought* becomes *sought, theorem* becomes *serum, think* becomes *sink,* and so on because there is a *si* in the Chinese *pinyin* transcript but not the voiceless /θ/. Or, instead of substituting /θ/ for /s/, they substitute /θ/ with a /t/ sound, as in *thank–tank, thin–tin.* This observation is in agreement with Chang (2001:311). Teaching Chinese learners to produce the voiceless /θ/ sound is difficult but can be done if they are shown the correct position of the tongue and given a lot of practice.

The other phonetic sound that is difficult for Chinese students is the nasal /ŋ/. Huang (1966) who studied the pronunciation problems of Cantonese speakers, attributes the failure of Chinese learners to pronounce /m/, /ŋ/ with the proper length because these sounds are extremely short in Chinese. Our PRC students normally substitute /ŋ/ with /n/ as in *sing–sin, rang–ran.* These are generally difficult for Cantonese and Fujian speakers because "when they occur at the end of a syllable and therefore are never 'released', i.e. for /n/ the tongue tip clings to the roof of the mouth; and for /ŋ/ the back of the tongue clings to the roof of the mouth. Cantonese and Fujian speakers will transfer these articulatory habits to English, and consequently these sounds seem to be 'swallowed'" (Kenworthy, 1998: 128).

However, in the questionnaire, 35% of CELC teachers do not agree that our students have a problem with /n/ and /ŋ/. This may be because /ŋ/ and /n/ were not taught as paired sounds, as in, *thin/thing* and *sin/sing* and these paired sentences which I used in class: "He doesn't want to sin. He doesn't want to sing", or a more difficult exercise like this, "Have you any thin silver? Have you anything silver?"(Barnard, 1979: 70). The problem with /ŋ/ is more obvious when paired with /n/, as /ŋ/ is a stressed fricative, but on its own poses little problem for most of our Chinese students. Generally, PRC students from any part of China have a serious problem with simple consonants such as /ŋ/ at the end of words, but when they do get the /ŋ/ right they can run into trouble pronouncing words like *singer* where the *ge* is over emphasised and becomes *sing-ge*. This is also a common problem with the postgraduate students from foreign universities not only from China but also Chinese students from the ASEAN countries.

Another fricative which can be difficult for some students is /ʃ/ which is substituted by the /s/ sound, as in *she–he, shop–sop, shoe–sue*. This habit is also noticeable among Cantonese and Fujian speakers (Kenworthy, 1998: 129). On the whole, CELC teachers do not think that /ʃ/ is easy (28.5%) while 35% disagree that there is any substitution of /s/ for /ʃ/. They think Chinese students cannot do *she*, for example, because in Chinese, the pronouns, *she* and *he* sound identical. Thus they believe Chinese students say *he* when they mean *she* and do not automatically transfer the /ʃ/ to /s/ as in *shop–sop, shoe–sue*. In general, /ʃ/ looks difficult to teach to some Chinese students but this problem can be overcome because in Mandarin there is a *sh* sound which is found in words such as *shi* or *shu* in *pinyin*. This observation is also made by Chang (2001: 312) who explained that /dz/, /tʃ/ and /ʃ/ are "distantly similar to a group of three different Chinese consonants". Although the Chinese tones are different (there are four tones in Mandarin), getting them to produce the Chinese sounds first and then keeping the shape of the lips (rounded and compressed) to produce the English sound is possible.

Less problematic in terms of accuracy are consonants such as /t/ and /d/, /f/ and /v/, /g/ and /k/, /p/ and /b/ although the difficulty varies from student to student. Mostly, they have a noticeable problem with these consonants which appear at the end of words. Problematic words are *rope–robe, cup–cub, nip–nib, heat–heed, fright–fried, slack–slag, flock–flog, leaf–leave, a life–alive.* Some of these problems are explained by Wu (1993) who said that in Mandarin, there are no voiced stops such as /b/, /d/, and /g/. Chinese students from Central China tend to give an extra sound to words ending with these consonants.

Problematic Vowels

Long sounds pose some problems for some learners, in particular /i:/ and /ɪ/ as in *sheep: ship*, /ɔ:/ as in *door, four*, and /ʊə/ as in *tour, sure,* which have no equivalent in the Chinese language. For instance, they tend to pronounce /ɪ/ and /ɪ/ so that one hears only *ship/ship* and not *sheep/ship*. They tend to add an extra sound to words with /ɔɪ/ ending in /l/ as in *soil-er* for *soil*.

Another noticeable habit among Chinese students is their habit of deleting or adding a syllable from two-syllabic words or more than two-syllabic words. This observation is in agreement with the findings of Li (1998) on a study of pronunciation problems of Taiwanese students. The most common pronunciation problem with the CELC students from Central China is adding another syllable to a monosyllabic word. What they are doing is to voice these consonants: /d/, /b/, /t/, /d/ and /k/. Thus words such as *and, should, must, but, job,* sound like: *and (de), should (de), must (te), but (te), job (ber).* Two-syllabic words such as *almost* becomes *al-mot-ter, college* becomes *co-lle-ge, knowledge* becomes *know-led-ge, village* becomes *vi-lla-ge* and so on. The Shandong students also have the same problem. It therefore sounds strange when these students read a sentence containing *and the* which is read as *and (de) the,* that is, three syllables. It is likely that this problem could have been caused by incorrect instruction in China, which teaches putting a voiced sound in voiceless consonants, and aspirating where aspiration is not necessary.

Polysyllabic words can have at least one syllable deleted by Chinese students. The above example, *generally,* is a good example because of the problem with /r/ and /l/ and sometimes with /n/ in the word.

Such an example is *revolution* which becomes *rev-lu-tion, everyone* becomes *ev-one, everything* becomes *ev-thing, dormitories* becomes *dorm-tories,* and so on. Possible explanations for such mispronunciation are careless reading, unfamiliarity with the vocabulary, the difficulty with words containing the problematic consonants (discussed above) and perhaps poor listening skills.

Specific Pronunciation Problems

Substituting /n/ for /l/ sound or vice versa is very common among students from Central China. Thus *technology* becomes *tech-lo-logy, underlying* becomes *under-nai-ing, recognised* becomes *recoglised,* and so on. Unlike the Northern Chinese students, some of these students tend to substitute /r/ for /l/ as in *grow–glow, rather–lather, arrangement–alangement, career–caleer* or *Korea* and so on.

It becomes complicated when students have to pronounce polysyllabic words containing both /n/ and /l/ as in *analytical* which becomes *a-la-ti-cal* dropping one syllable or, it sometimes gets pronounced as *a-na-na-ti-cal,* keeping all the syllables but pronouncing only the /n/ sounds. The cause of this problem could have arisen from the way these students were taught Chinese pronunciation, or it could be the interference of mother tongue. This observation is also made by Chan and Li who explained that Cantonese speakers of English tend to substitute /l/ for /n/ as they do in Cantonese, substituting *l* for *n,* because there is only the pre-vocalic clear *l* which exists in Cantonese sound, i.e. before vowels (as in the English word *live*), and "substituting *l* for *n* neutralises their opposition; but such variations rarely give rise to communication problems for the intended meaning may usually be disambiguated by the context" (Chan and Li, 2000: 80). Although the Cantonese-speaking students in this survey did not have such an obvious problem it was more noticeable among the Central Chinese students. One of our PRC teachers explains that in certain parts of China, Sichuan for example, the *l* in the *pinyin* transcript is pronounced as *n.* Thus a word like "dragon" which is transcribed as *long* will be pronounced as *nong* by these students. I tested this out with more Chinese words such as *nai* (endurance) which was pronounced as *lai,* and *nuan* (warm) pronounced as *luan* instead. However, not all Chinese words transcribed with /n/ are pronounced with the /l/ sound and vice versa. But because of fossilised learning some Chinese students somehow transferred the /l/ and /n/ sound in Mandarin to most English words containing /l/ and /n/.

An interesting observation is that the *pinyin r* which used to be pronounced as *y* by Chinese living in the province of Liaoning, Jilin and Heilonjiang as well as the older overseas Chinese (Lin, 1991:371) does not present the same kind of pronunciation problem for our students. For example, *rong yi* meaning "easy" in *pinyin* used to be pronounced as *yong yi* before *pinyin* was invented, and *rang* (let) used to be pronounced as *yang*; similarly, *yong*, meaning "military" is now *rong*. The author Jung Chang (which is the anglicised transcription of Chinese sounds) of the "Wild Swans" fame used the old transcription of *yong* though now she is known as Zhang Rong by Chinese-speaking people.

The Southern Chinese students in this survey seem to have the least problems with English pronunciation. However, their main error is in substituting /v/ for /b/ as in *activity–actibity* and /v/ for /w/ as in: *everyvhere* for *everywhere*. 69% of CELC teachers agree that Chinese students confuse /v/ for /w/ and vice versa. A possible explanation for this is that both sound alike mainly because /v/ is a consonant, while /w/ may sound either like a consonant or semi-vowel. Otherwise their problems are quite common with most foreign learners of English, for example, *advertisement–ad-ver-tice-ment, relatives–ri-latives, vacation–vocation,* and enunciation problems such as *like–lie* (k missing), *climbing–cli-bing* (m missing), *class–cass* (1 missing).

Mispronunciation such as these can be attributed to either poor teaching in China (Feng, 2000; Wong and Lopez, 2000: 279) or the lack of emphasis on oral skills (Dzau, 1990). Sometimes even when learners become aware of the errors, learn to identify them and to correct themselves, they may slip into the old habit of mispronouncing. But in an English-speaking environment like Singapore the pre-matriculation students from PRC need to be more accurate in their speaking skills to communicate well in a multi-cultural society.

TEACHING APPLICATIONS

To help these students improve their speaking skills, it is necessary to start with pronunciation drills. Teaching pronunciation strategies will vary depending on the types of students we have but CELC teachers have indicated that some of the following strategies may be useful:

- Using similar sounds in Mandarin wherever possible
- Teaching placement of tongue, lips, teeth, etc.
- Providing self-access to listening tapes
- Training students to listen and identify own errors or errors of other students
- Providing exercises in tongue-twisters
- Providing articulation exercises using funny poems, children's rhythms & rhymes
- Encouraging students to listen to the radio, for example, BBC or watch TV
- Scheduling more classroom practice in minimal pairs monitored by teacher.

The above teaching tips, which are not exhaustive, reflect the trial-and-tested approach used with a group size of about 20 students. They would have been used by CELC teachers whose main concern must have been the learning ability and needs of individual student as well as their motivational levels. These reflect the general teaching practice recommendations of academics such as Strevens (1991: 103) and Kelly (2000). They are also modelled on the innovative and creative strategies such as using tongue-twisters (Ur, 1997: 54), rhymes and poetry (Goodwin, 2001) as well as learner autonomy through learner diaries (Seidlhofer, 2001: 63–64), which have been discussed by my CELC colleagues in this book on learning strategies of PRC students. However, none of the above tips included pronunciation games (Hancock, 1995), which for some reason or other, were not used by CELC tutors, who might have other preferences of methodology in teaching pronunciation; nor did they use jazz chants (Graham 1978; Ur, 1997: 54) which required the PRC students to be familiar with the rhythm of jazz but which, apparently, they were not, and so these pronunciation activities were not introduced in the classroom. This is not to say that PRC students would not be able to enjoy such pronunciation activities. They, as well as the postgraduate students, were responsive to the use of poems with rhythm and rhymes to teach pronunciation (Ho, 2001).

Generally, it is observable that all Chinese learners of English, regardless of whether they are competent or weak in speaking skills, are enthusiastic about improving their pronunciation. The above-mentioned teaching strategies of pronunciation have also been recommended by others such as Seidlhofer (2001: 62–64) who discussed 8 different teaching and learning strategies, and should be stimulating and interesting for such learners. However, considering the cultural and educational background of the PRC students the following pointers/strategies are ranked, starting with the most important.

- Knowledge in Mandarin and even some of the Southern Chinese dialects such as Cantonese and Fujian, is an advantage. It is possible to help learners transfer some of the Mandarin sounds to English. For instance, the pinyin *shi* can be used to teach /ʃ/.
- Knowledge of not only Mandarin sounds but Chinese culture can help the teacher decide the best teaching methodology. For example, classroom practice in minimal pairs monitored by the teacher may work better instead of one-to-one teaching involving individual student with the teacher, which may intimidate some students. Culturally, Chinese learners are more familiar with large group teaching with little interaction between teacher and students thereby diffusing class attention on individual students (Nelson, 1995). Knowing this will help teachers to decide the best kind of language activities in class. Teaching the placement of tongue, teeth, lips, etc. to produce the correct sounds may be more difficult with Chinese learners as some may feel embarrassed or shy about performing such actions. However, once this cultural barrier is overcome (when the students are more familiar with the teaching styles in our English classes) it should be easy to teach pronunciation more effectively.
- A very effective way of teaching pronunciation to PRC students is to videotape the students presenting an oral talk, either in an informal or formal situation or participate in story-telling sessions. Though the purpose of a videotaped oral presentation is to teach good delivery techniques at this Centre it can be effective in identifying the pronunciation problems of individual students who can then see and hear for themselves why they may not sound intelligible. Many of the PRC students in CELC, including the postgraduate students, who never had the experience of seeing themselves "perform" on the television screen, are often spurred

to improve, having had the preconceived idea that their speaking skills were reasonably good. Videotaping oral presentation is so time-consuming that there may not be time for other classroom activities but it is worth the time and effort as nothing beats "seeing and hearing" as a form of self, peer and teacher feedback.

• Another factor is the duration of the pronunciation lesson. The lack of time devoted to teaching this skill is certainly a problem in achieving success in teaching pronunciation. Thus with English proficiency courses that span 12 weeks it is necessary to concentrate only on the most difficult pronunciation problems. The less problematic pronunciation sounds will have to be dealt with by the students themselves who could be directed to self-access learning facilities and materials that are available and accessible to students. There are any number of audiotapes, VCD movies and even CD-ROMs on learning English pronunciation in the market nowadays, as well as resources for both teachers and learners of pronunciation on the Internet where the list of pronunciation websites can be found (Goodwin, 2001: 129) but ultimately, it is the teacher's responsibility to recommend the most suitable titles or programmes to meet the needs of the students.

• With the pre-matriculation students from China it is possible to see some improvement in their pronunciation after 6 months of intensive English learning. During this time the most important teaching strategy is to make the learners become aware of their problems, identify the mistakes and be able to correct their errors themselves. This exercise need not be monitored by the teacher; instead, the students should be assigned to do this outside class with a partner and a test can be then conducted by the teacher as a follow-up activity. The ability to listen and identify errors is crucial in any pronunciation learning and if students can succeed in doing this, any follow-up teaching will be easier. This awareness and self-feedback is the key to successful pronunciation as Harmer (Harmer, 2001: 185) also notes. Unfortunately, training students to listen for their own errors is very time-consuming and labour-intensive as it necessitates individual coaching — listening to the student's errors, identifying each error, correcting it and training the student to do the same, and with the aid of audio equipment and materials. Such a teaching strategy can be used on a less frequent basis with large groups of students.

- In classroom teaching it is not necessary to teach pronunciation as a special lesson; rather it can be taught whenever appropriate but it must form a component of the language activity. Using a language laboratory should facilitate the teaching of pronunciation but the lessons and drills should not be tediously long. Sometimes pronunciation lessons may give rise to boredom to those who are quite good, especially female students, if the teacher concentrates too much on the weaker ones. One solution to this problem is to teach the weaker students outside class hours or alternatively to give self-access learning materials. With a large class size of 20 for instance, it is difficult trying to achieve good results. It will be more effective teaching few students at a time, which can be done while the rest of the class is involved in other non-oral language activities.

The above observation of pronunciation teaching strategies concurs with others such as those of Ur (1997), Parish (1991), Harmer (2001) and Seidlhofer (2001) but with PRC students at CELC, a sensitive approach is proposed to provide more effective learning strategies. An important consideration is to introduce some humour by the teacher who can also inject some "fun" element in the teaching activities. Students on their parts, could make learning interesting if they could cultivate a sense of humour — their ability to laugh at themselves, at their poor pronunciation. This would save them from the embarrassment of consistently making the same horrendous mistakes, which, if not salvaged, could be a de-motivating factor for even the least sensitive student. Most of all, a positive attitude and a determination to improve must come from the students themselves. This, together with an acceptance of a teaching style totally different from those used in China, should help PRC students improve their English pronunciation to some degree of intelligibility. These observations were made from teaching PRC students since 1996 but there may be exceptions to the rule, depending on the personalities of the learners as well as the teaching style and activities by individual teachers.

SUMMARY

Although pronunciation problems can vary from individual student to individual student from any region of China, the most acute problems in this study are with /r/, /l/ /ŋ/, the fricative /θ/, either at the beginning or end of words, and /ɔ:/ since there is no such sound in Chinese. More accurate sounds can be produced with diphthongs and vowels. Most PRC students have few problems with /v/, as in *veal*, /f/ as in *feel*, /w/ as in *war*, /m/ as in *mouse, summer*, /h/ as in *house*, /t/ as in *chin, coach*, and /p/ and /b/, /t/ and /d/, /k/ and /g/ at the beginning of words as in *pig–big, ten–den, could–good*.

It is generally difficult to concentrate on all phonetic sounds to help improve the pronunciation problems of PRC students but this study has attempted to identify the most difficult ones. There may be different observations made in other studies compared to this study but from our observation, the students who come from the coastal cities such as Shanghai and Guangdong tend to have better speaking skills and more accurate pronunciation as they may have more exposure to Western media such as cable television. Similarly, students who have attended English lessons conducted by native English speakers in China have better speaking skills. As this was a small-scale survey, further investigation will be needed to verify the above findings. On the whole, the findings of this survey would help teachers of PRC students become more aware of their specific pronunciation weaknesses and to devise various teaching styles and materials best suited to the learning needs of these students.

REFERENCES

Abercombie, D. (1991). Teaching pronunciation. In Adam Brown (Ed.), *Teaching English Pronunciation* (pp. 87–95). London: Routledge.

Barale, C. (1982). *A Quantitative Analysis of the Loss of Final Consonants in Beijing Mandarin.* Ph.D thesis. Michigan: University of Pennsylvania.

Barnard, G. & McKay, P.S. (1979). *Practice in Spoken English: An Anthology of Exercises in English Sounds.* Illustrated by Jennetta Vise. London: Macmillan.

Chan, Y.W. & Li, C.S. (2000). English and Cantonese phonology in contrast: Explaining Cantonese ESL learners' English pronunciation problems. *Language, Culture and Curriculum*, 13(1): 67–85.

Chang, J. (2001). Chinese speakers. In M. Swan & B. Smith (Eds.), *Learner English: A Teacher's Guide to Interference and Other Problems*, 2nd edition (pp. 310–24). Cambridge: Cambridge University Press.

Dzau, Y.F. (1990). How English is taught in tertiary educational institutions. In Y.F.Dzau (Ed.), *English in China* (pp. 41–58). Hong Kong: API Press.

Feng, A.W. (1999). *ELT in Chinese tertiary institutions — Amazing facts, culture of learning and pedagogical implications.* Paper presented at the Centre for English Language Communication, May, National University of Singapore, Singapore.
_____ (2000). *The culture learners bring to the classroom — An easily neglected essential.* Paper presented at the Centre for English Language Communication, November, National University of Singapore, Singapore.

Flege, J. E. (1980). Transfer and developmental processes in adult foreign language speech production. *Applied Psycholinguistics,* 5: 323–47.

Graham, C. (1978). *Jazz Chants.* Oxford: Oxford University Press.

Goodwin, J. (2001). Teaching pronunciation. In Marianne Celce-Murcia (Ed.), *Teaching English as a Second or Foreign Language,* 3rd edition (pp. 117–33). U.S.: Heinle & Heinle.

Hancock, M. (1995). *Pronunciation Games.* Cambridge: Cambridge University Press.

Harmer, J. (2001). *The Practice of English Language Teaching,* 3rd edition. Essex, England: Longman.

Ho, L. (2001). Rhythm and Rhymes: A different approach to teaching pronunciation to PRC adult learners. Paper presented at the *International Language in Education Conference,* Hong Kong, 13–15 December.

Hockett, C.F. (1972). Learning pronunciation. In Croft (Ed.), *Reading on English as a Second Language.* Cambridge, MA: Winthrop Publishers, Inc.

Huang, R. (1966). *English Pronunciation Explained with Diagrams.* London: Oxford University Press.

Huang, Agnes L. (1998). Auditory perception of word-final voiceless sounds in listening tasks. In *Proceedings of the 7th International Symposium on English Teaching,* Volume 1(pp. 467–75).

Kelly, G. (2000). *How to Teach Pronunciation,* Essex, England: Pearson Education Press.

Kenworthy, J. (1998). *Teaching English Pronunciation.* 3rd edition. London: Longman.

Lado, R. (1957). *Linguistics Across Cultures.* Ann Arbor: The University of Michigan Press.

Li, C.Y. (1998).The problems Chinese learners have in pronouncing English consonant sounds. *Proceedings of the 7th International Symposium on English Teaching,* Taipei, Volume 2 (pp. 639–47).

Lin, T. (1991). The scope of Pekingese. In Wang, S.Y. (Ed.), *Journal of Chinese Linguistics.* Monograph series No. 3 (pp. 363–76). California: University of California, Berkeley.

Nelson, G. (1995). Cultural differences in learning styles. In Joy Reid (Ed.), *Learning Styles in the ESL Classroom* (pp. 3–18). Boston: Heinle & Heinle.

Parish, C. (1991). A practical philosophy of pronunciation. In Adam Brown (Ed.), *Teaching English Pronunciation* (pp. 104–112). London: Routledge.

Ramsey, J. (1987). *The Languages of China.* Princeton: Princeton University Press.

Seidlhofer, B. (2001). Pronunciation. In Ronald Carter and David Nunan (Eds.), *The Cambridge Guide to Teaching English to Speakers of Other Languages* (pp. 56–65). Cambridge: Cambridge University Press.

Strevens, P. (1991). A rationale for teaching pronunciation: The rival virtues of innocence and sophistication. In Adam Brown (Ed.), *Teaching English Pronunciation* (pp. 96–103). London: Routledge.

Ting, P.H. (1991). Some theoretical issues in the study of Mandarin dialects. In Wang, S.Y. (Ed.), *Journal of Chinese Linguistics,* Monograph series No. 3 (pp. 187–236). California: University of California, Berkeley.

Ur, P. (1997). *A Course in Language Teaching.* Cambridge: Cambridge University Press.

Wu, N.C. (1993). A contrastive study of Mandarin Chinese and American English phonological systems. *Journal of Taipei Business Junior College*, 41: 361–465.

Wong, S.L. and Lopez, M.G. (2000). English language learners of Chinese background. In Lee McKay and Wong, S.L. (Eds.), *New Immigrants in the United States* (pp. 263–305). Cambridge: Cambridge University Press.

APPENDIX A. PRONUNCIATION PROBLEMS TRANSCRIBED FROM VIDEOTAPED ORAL PRESENTATIONS

South China (Guangzhou, Shenzhen)

while — *whie* /l/ missing
class — *cass*
like — *lie* /k/ missing
climbing — *clibing* /m/ missing
relatives — *rilatives*
mountain — *mountein*
holiday — *halliday*
activity — *actibity*
everywhere — *everyvhere/ev-vhere*
village — *vil-la-ge* (3 syllables)
dormitories — *dormtrories* (3 syllables)
students — *stdents* (1 syllable)

North China (Beijing, Shandong)

everyone — *evrrone* (stress on "rr")
usually — *urrually*
must–*must-te* (2 syllables)
think — *think-er* (2 syllables)
great — *gret-te* (2 syllables)
subject — *subjet-te* (3 syllables)
almost — *almot-te* (3 syllables)
college — *col-le-ge* (3 syllables)
normally — *norm-ly* (2 syllables)
satisfied — *sat-fied* (2 syllables)
share — *shell* /r/ missing

Central China (Shanghai, Hangzhou)

world — *word* /l/ missing
everything — *ev'thing* /r/ and /v/ missing
experience — *experance*
attitude — *alttitude* /l/ added

career — *caleer*
warmth — *warm* /th/ missing
fireworks — *fiworks* /r/ missing (2 syllables)
lunar — *lular*
snow — *slow*

Central China (Hubei, Henan, Sichuan)

technology — *tech-lo-lo-gy*
knowledge — *low-led-ge* (3 syllables)
evening — *eve-ling*
arrangement — *a-lange-ment*
know — *low*
not — *lot*
level — *nevel*
needs — *leeds*
enough — *elough*
natural — *latural*
nowadays — *lowadays*
another — *anlather*
rather — *lather*
grow — *glow*
zero — *dero*
clothes — *cloth-es* (2 syllables)
much — *much-er* (2 syllables)
is — *i-iz* (2 syllables)
first — *first-te* (2 syllables)
job — *job-ber*
and — *and-de*
eggs — *egg-es*
should — *should-de*
results — *resuts* /l/ missing
introduce — *int-duce* (2 syllables)
everyone — *evr'one* (2 syllables)
usually — *ujually*
knowledge — *knowledge-ge* (3 syllables)
revolution — *rev-lution* (3 syllables)
secondly — *secondarly* (4 syllables)

CHAPTER 10

Strategy Training for English Language Learners from PRC

SUSAN TAN

INTRODUCTION

In the last two decades applied linguists, language teachers and educationists have been earnestly seeking to better understand how language learners learn and how they can be taught to learn better. This desire to nurture autonomous learners has led to numerous studies to help language learners be more self-directed, proactive, goal-oriented, creative and independent. Extensive research (reviewed below) has gone into discovering how good language learners manage their learning and how students can be taught to better manage their learning to obtain maximum effect.

Training or teaching students about the techniques, or more precisely, the strategies of language learning can be highly beneficial especially in situations where students are in a language programme for only a short time. Many students are unable to continue on their own with language learning once classes end. If these students are equipped with the means and knowledge to self-direct and manage their own learning beyond the classroom then they can continue to learn independently of their teacher. Successful language learning may rest on this autonomy.

This chapter describes a classroom research study that investigated the effects of teaching language learning strategies to foreign graduate students enrolled in the Graduate English course at the Centre for English Language Communication (CELC, NUS). The aims of strategy training in these classes were to help these foreign language students become more aware of the strategies they could use to learn more effectively, to monitor and to evaluate their learning process.

This research hypothesises that language learners who received strategy training would develop a greater awareness of their language learning processes. When the learners are given the opportunity to reflect meaningfully about their learning, they would begin to discover more ways to learn, understand more about the importance of employing strategies and be more self-directed and more goal-oriented in their language study.

LITERATURE OVERVIEW

A survey of articles on learner strategy research reveals that many writers trace the beginnings to the changing focus of classrooms, from a teacher-centred to a learner-centred one. This focus on the learner and the identification of learner needs in relation to learning a language is underpinned by the educational goal of equipping learners to be more involved in the process of learning.

In 1975, two landmark articles concerned with the identification of the characteristics of the effective language learner were written (Stern, 1975; Rubin, 1975). These studies revealed that effective learners employed a variety of learning strategies and these strategies were subsequently described and classified (Rubin, 1981, 1987; Rubin & Thompson, 1982; O'Malley & Chamot, 1990; Oxford, 1990).

Various definitions of learning strategies have been offered. Wenden (1987) describes them as learning behaviours involving strategic knowledge as well as knowledge about learning. Learners use them to learn and to regulate learning. Oxford (1990) considers them as specific actions that are used for the purpose of making learning faster, easier, more enjoyable, more self-directed, more effective and more transferable to new situations. In a more recent article she writes that "All language learning strategies are related to the features of control, goal-directedness, autonomy and self-efficacy" (Oxford 2001: 166).

The common strand that runs through the various definitions offered is that learning strategies are specific processes that a learner consciously selects in order to help him in his learning.

O'Malley and Chamot (1990) describe strategies as cognitive processes and they have classified the list of identified strategies into 3 categories. Metacognitive strategies are those that involve planning for, monitoring or evaluating a learning activity. Cognitive strategies, on the other hand, "involve manipulation of the material to be learned" (Chamot, 1987: 72).

These strategies are used to help understanding and memory. The last category of strategies is social and affective strategies and these help the learner to learn by getting help from others and by lowering the affective filter within himself. Rubin (1987) classifies metacognitive and cognitive strategies as strategies that directly affect learning whereas social strategies do not.

Language learning strategy research has proven fruitful in identifying and classifying a host of potentially useful strategies. The applied focus of this research is to compare strategies that are used by successful and less successful language learners. With this understanding teachers could provide instruction or training in the relevant strategies to help learners to become more successful.

Wenden (1991) links strategy use to the concept of learner autonomy in that through strategy use the learner takes responsibility for her learning and develops strategies for doing so. McDonough commented on the increased use of the term 'learner strategies', a change from the more restricted term 'learning strategies' (McDonough, 1999). McDonough is of the opinion that the term 'learner strategies' places greater emphasis on the learner as an active participant in the learning process. The learner is a problem solver and reflective organiser. There seems to be an assumption that when learners become more involved in the learning process they become autonomous learners. This is reflected in Oxford's comment that "learning strategies help learners become autonomous" (2001: 166).

The concept of learner autonomy is a complex field and extends to areas like curriculum design. It would take a much more extensive review of the literature to do it justice. In the limited context of this research, the concept of autonomy simply means that learners are more able to self-manage their learning through setting learning goals, selecting learning strategies and monitoring progress.

Learners who receive strategy training generally learn better than those who do not. A review of developmental studies on learning strategies concludes that learning strategies "develop with age, are used spontaneously with increasing sophistication by older students, result in improved task performance and can be taught" (O'Malley & Chamot, 1990: 106).

For this reason, most studies on strategy training have involved mature students in high schools or tertiary institutions. Training with such students has yielded favourable results (Cohen & Aphek, 1980; O'Malley et al., 1985; Chamot, 1993; Cohen, Weaver and Li, 1996; Nunan, 1996; Wenden, 1996).

O'Malley et al. (1985) conducted an experimental study of the effectiveness of strategy training with students of English as a second language which focused on three types of academic tasks: vocabulary learning, listening comprehension and oral production. Results showed that in the skills of listening and speaking, strategy training was effective in enhancing initial learning. Other work has been done on the training of specific strategies for vocabulary learning (Cohen & Aphek, 1980).

Cohen et al. (1996) conducted a research study with university level foreign language classrooms which had a particular focus on speaking. In this study, foreign language students were assessed to determine if strategies-based instruction affected speaking performance. They found that those students who received strategy instruction outperformed the control group who did not receive similar instruction. Nunan (1996) found that strategy training, plus the systematic provision of opportunities for learners to reflect on the learning process, led to greater sensitivity to the learning process over time. The study found, inter alia, that at the end of the course the participating students were more likely to use opportunities that existed for learning and use beyond the classroom than they were at the beginning.

RESEARCH SETUP

The 24 learners who received strategy training instruction were among those enrolled in the Intermediate Level Graduate English Course, which is one among the special English courses conducted by CELC. The course adopts a multi-skills approach with the aim to raise the English proficiency of students to a level that allows them to communicate with fluency and accuracy in formal and informal situations and in practical, social, academic and professional areas. They were placed into two classes of 12 each following the analysis of the oral proficiency scores obtained from a diagnostic test. Group

A was classified as being in the upper intermediate range, while group B was in the lower intermediate range.

All the learners are from the People's Republic of China. Most of them were between 24 and 30 years old; only one was 41 years of age. Nineteen had been in Singapore for no more than three months at the commencement of the English course. Five had worked in Singapore for a few months before enrolling as graduate students in NUS.

The learners were introduced to and trained in the use of learning strategies during the course of their regular English classes which were conducted twice a week over 12 weeks, totalling 48 hours. As far as possible, strategy training was integrated with the course curriculum and materials. Training in strategies was explicit, i.e. each strategy was named and identified to the learners. Although individual strategies were emphasised during a particular lesson, most activities required the use of more than one strategy for their completion. This ensured that learners were exposed to multiple strategies, as research evidence has shown that good language learners have a wide repertoire of learning strategies and use a variety of strategies in any learning task (O'Malley & Chamot, 1990).

Learners were asked to maintain weekly entries in their learning diaries using cues as prompts to help them to examine their learning progress and to make learning plans for the coming week. The format of the learning diary is the same as that used in Nunan's (1996) study of tertiary level students learning English in Hong Kong. A sample is reproduced in Appendix A. The data in the diary was used to see how strategy training had affected their personal learning methods, awareness of difficulties and goals for learning. These diaries were examined and recorded by the author every few weeks. Learners were told of the possible benefits that could be gained from the exercise though no extra credits would be earned and their participation was entirely voluntary.

RESULTS AND DISCUSSION

As training was provided in metacognitive, cognitive, social and affective strategies, diary entries were examined to see if learners had used or developed these strategies.

From the diary entries, it was evident that learners had discovered new ways to learn. They had increasingly definite ideas about the methods they could use to learn as the weeks went by. Compare Student A's entry in the first week to her entry in the later weeks:

> 1st week : "only way for me to improve ... is to practice more ..."
>
> 5th week : "talking with Indian or Singaporean students, reading newspapers, watching TV and movies, listening to radio ... review the book, 'The Secrets of English Words' ... tells us how to remember words by the roots (prefix and suffix)."
>
> 8th week : "... telling stories is also a good way to improve spoken English."

Student A showed increasing sophistication about the ways she could learn English. Her methods and plans became more definite. She discussed new vocabulary with colleagues and started to learn the morphology of English words as a method for vocabulary learning. She found that she enjoyed story telling as a way to practise spoken English so she started to analyse how story telling could be done well:

> 10th week: "before you tell a story you must think over what you want to say ... and what's the main idea ... organize the whole ... arrange the ideas ... think over how to express it in the easiest way so that everyone can understand ... lastly ... better to use some humorous method ..."

Not only did this student find new ways to learn, she also used such opportunities to improve her learning. She made increasingly definite and sophisticated plans to gain more from each method.

Student E recorded that in class he learned new vocabulary learning strategies, which he had not used before. In the following week he wrote that he found it easier to understand new words with the help of sample sentences. He also noticed that when he learnt new words in certain contexts he could remember them more easily. This led to a plan to learn words in groups according to the context in which they appeared. For instance, he found that he could remember the words he learned on financial news from newspapers as he prepared to do a short talk on the Asian financial crisis.

Some students became more systematic in learning new vocabulary. They categorised new words learned and learned to put new words in a sentence. Vocabulary learning at the sentence level appeared to help them in understanding and recall. Student G tried to learn new vocabulary by recalling all the words that were related to the new word. He found that there were two benefits to this method as it helped him to learn a new word as well as to review other words he had learned. This student's reflection seems to confirm Carter's observation on how vocabulary is acquired. He notes that vocabulary items learned in context were better retained and that having more processes involved in the learning of a word usually translates to better retention and recall (Carter, 2001).

There was a change too in learners' attitudes to learning new words. Often these students would be eager to learn difficult and sophisticated vocabulary. However, they found that they had difficulty finding occasions to use such words and they also had trouble trying to recall their meanings. This resulted in frustration for the students. So, it was pleasant to note that as the weeks went by, many of them were also beginning to learn useful vocabulary, rather than difficult but rarely used words. For instance, one student learned the word 'paroxysm' but lamented that she had no opportunity to use it. Some weeks later she noted that the word 'envelop' could be used both as a noun and as a verb with a slight change of spelling. She noted that simple words could be more useful to her.

Student F learned to get more out of reading professional texts. In the 2nd week he recorded that he did not know how to learn language from such kinds of materials. In the 5th week, after a training task on concept mapping to get main ideas from reading passages, he wrote:

> "I studied an article … many new words … when I read it a second time I understood more … tried to draw a concept map … the main idea displayed itself to me very clearly. I find it an effective way to read scientific paper."

This student had learned a strategy that he found transferable to other learning situations.

For other students, there was growing awareness that a previous learning method might not be good. Student M planned to change his learning technique to suit his learning style, which was apparently more visual.

5th week : "I have changed my habit of learning English. When I encounter a new word, not only learn its meaning and usage, but also learn its spelling. I think only when I spell it well and use it freely do I really understand this new word."

Another significant area where learners showed increasing sensitivity was in the way they evaluated learning techniques. There was evidence that their beliefs about the way to learn affected their choice of learning methods. In addition, they were beginning to see language learning more as a process and less as a product.

Student D started the first week wanting to know a quicker way to improve her English. In the 3rd week she recorded that "language learning is a period of practice". In the 6th week she acknowledged that language learning was not "course work". She was also able to evaluate suggested learning methods. She felt that a classmate's idea to use Chinese subtitles to understand English movies was not a good idea because to her it was using "a language stick" and the method would encourage her to "do translation in your brain". She also concluded that watching documentaries on Chinese culture in English was not a good idea. Although the familiar topic would make for easier understanding, she felt that language was not learnt through the language in itself but also through its culture. "Only by understanding the cultural background of western world do we learn foreign language better." This student harboured personal beliefs about language and these beliefs affected her choice of ways to learn. She rejected the methods that were unappealing and seemingly incorrect to her. She also came to realize that fluency was not everything. Her 9th week entry reads:

"Previously I thought that speaking is a proud thing. I found I would make a lot of stupid mistakes. Therefore I changed my idea and planned to speak slowly and thoughtfully."

After the first week of lessons, Student G recorded that he learned how to identify information words (keywords) in an English sentence. He felt that this strategy of selectively attending to important information was "very useful since my brain is slow when it process English information ... processing speed will be increased if it can concentrate on the information words".

Learners were also more astute in evaluating their studying/learning progress. This was an important development because many students often felt discouraged and frustrated at some point in their study by their seeming lack of improvement.

Student M was conscious of the difference between the first time he had to speak at length in class and the second time he did so. He felt that he was more fluent and he wrote:

> "that is the progress we have made ... by now, I am willing to speak English. And I dare to open my mouth. No matter how many mistakes ... I can say some English. I am glad I have made such progress."

Student H too, reported progress in listening and reading skills. In the first week she found listening to BBC "not easy" while reading novels was "very difficult". In the 6th week she had progressed sufficiently to report that she found the daily practice of listening to BBC had made it easier to understand. In the 10th week, she recorded her improved reading ability:

> "... read English novel ... when I was eager to know the result of the story, my reading speed is very fast and I can guess many words. I didn't check the dictionary for one time ... popular novels are easy for me ... author only use normal words ... I can totally understand the meaning."

In this segment Student H was beginning to show evidence that perservering in her learning and that though she could not comprehend fully she felt a certain sense of achievement so long as she could guess at the meanings of unfamiliar vocabulary. She also realised that these unfamiliar words need not necessarily impede her understanding nor her reading pace. This helped her to finish her reading quickly and encouraged her to read more.

A significant observation was that learners were beginning to be more astute at monitoring their production. Student C began the course by making quite general statements like "I speak too fast and cause a lot of grammar problems." In his 5th week entry, he noted that he had started to check himself more carefully by using a tape recorder and found that he could identify many mistakes on the tape. By around the 7th week he was able to pinpoint specific errors:

"I did not use the past tense ... in my speaking ... past tense is
always in the wrong place ... while writing ... different kinds of
word tenses are mixed ... in my speaking I always use he or him
to a female and she or her to a male."

This was an important development as many students felt that the
teacher was the only person who could identify their mistakes.

Student F discerned the value of being accurate in order to convey
one's meaning more clearly. He reported that while travelling in a taxi
to go for a meeting, he had said, "We'll be there on time" and his Indian
colleague corrected him by saying, "in time". Student F wrote, "He
expressed more clearly than I, because we arrived there 15 minutes
in advance."

Student J reported that he was surprised by the negative feedback
on his pronunciation from fellow students after his first short oral
presentation. He thought he had pronounced well and could not
understand the difference between his assessment and the assessment
of his classmates. He felt that maybe this was because "we cannot
judge what we have done by ourselves" because the same brain controls
both processes — acting and observing one's actions at the same time.
However, he learned later that he was able to monitor his production
during his class presentation, for he wrote in the 6th week:

"... not as good as what I expected. I forgot to use 'turmoil, drop,
fluctuate' ... it is not easy to speak in English ..."

In addition he was able to judge that his topic on currency fluctuations
in Asia was very wide so he should have narrowed it down to make
it easier to handle. It was a promising development to note that he was
able to evaluate his performance in order to seek better ways to
approach it.

The diary entries also revealed that learners were practising and
using the strategy of selective attention to regulate their learning and
use of language. Student S had reported in the 1st week that listening
was a problem for him. In the 3rd week, he wrote that he was able
to understand an Indian colleague who speaks fast by concentrating
on keywords. Other learners also reported that they could understand

most of what they heard on the radio or TV by grasping the general meaning though they could not understand every word.

Diary entries were also examined to see if learners were utilising the cognitive strategies they learnt in class. The analysis shows that learners were beginning to use the strategies of inferencing, prediction and attending to context to help them to understand the English language.

In the 6th week, Student G wrote that he watched the movie 'A Farewell To Arms', but found the quality of the video very poor. Yet he managed to understand the plot because he had read the blurb on the cover of the video before watching the tape. He concluded:

"... so I think that it's important to get some useful information as hints, introduction before you watch a film, attend English lecture. It will help you on what the speaker said."

Lastly, the diaries were scrutinised to find out if the learners had used any social and affective strategies in their language learning. In this area the entries revealed that the learners had actively sought out people to help them in their learning. Many learners initially lamented that their language environment was poor as there were few native speakers around them. Most learners also spent their after-office hours with their own countrymen. As the weeks passed, more learners started to record that they were seeking out Indian colleagues to practise with. The Indian students, though not native speakers themselves, have much better oral skills.

Learners were using colleagues, spouses, even neighbours to help them practise their language. Learners were apparently making more self-directed efforts at managing their own learning by creating more opportunities to learn and by turning to their friends as language resources and language partners.

Student H reported receiving help from her fellow students when they taught her how to answer questions in detail. She sought out a learning partner who lived in the same hostel but she was not optimistic about the chances of improving her English as she felt that the girl had the same level of proficiency as hers. Fortunately, she came to realise that her friend's listening comprehension was better, so they watched TV together and discussed the content afterwards. Additionally, learners were also engaged in more positive self-talk. Few improvements were noted and progress was celebrated.

RESEARCH AND PEDAGOGICAL IMPLICATIONS

The strategy training offered in this study appears to have helped the learners to gain an increased measure of control, goal-directedness, autonomy and self-efficacy in their language learning processes (Oxford, 2001). They had become more active participants in the learning process as suggested by McDonough (1999). Learners had become more sophisticated at fine-tuning their plans for learning. There was more initiative in managing learning and general and vague plans for learning became more concrete and specific. Learners were planning more in order to get the results they wanted.

Results also indicate that the learners were beginning to evaluate their learning methods. This process involves recognising the need to change old styles and habits as well as to clear up misconceptions about learning. Their personal choices about learning methods affected their selection of ways to learn. Some learners realised that they had to be willing to change and to attempt different methods to get better results. This was especially true for these students from the PRC. From personal interviews regarding their learning background and expectations, as well as class observation, I gathered that students expected the teacher to do all the leading in class and to answer all their questions. In China, these students had learned English in teacher-centred classrooms where communicative interaction, whether between student and teacher or student and student, was very limited. Pair and group work in class were not familiar to them. So these students were initially very hesitant about group and pair work and some even wrote in their learning diary that they would like the teacher to talk to them on an individual basis. They were not comfortable with the idea of learning from their peers. Only through many sessions of co-operative work were they convinced of the importance and usefulness of social strategies and interactions in their language learning.

As a result, learners also became increasingly creative in sourcing practice opportunities as well as language resources. They were better able to monitor their production and to view them not as evidence of failure but as learning opportunities. This increased ability to make plans, to seek out opportunities and ways to learn, to evaluate and monitor production had apparently helped these learners to see their language learning as being holistic. When their learning goals were fulfilled they were able to congratulate themselves. Small strides became evident when they were detailed and recorded.

By using cognitive strategies like attending to more important information and keywords, inferring, predicting and guessing, they learned to make language learning more manageable. This is important to students who 'suffer' from information overload because they have to live in a new environment and use a foreign language.

The act of recording occasions when they spoke to others in English and plans they made to seek out opportunities to speak had the effect of actually spurring them on to actualise these plans. Similar results were reported in Nunan's study in Hong Kong (Nunan, 1996).

As NUS continues to draw an increasing pool of foreign graduate students from non-English medium universities, there is a need to source for and implement the methods that will optimise student learning in our 12-week language course. There is an acute need to prepare the learners to manage and regulate their own learning. Most of these graduate students have excelled in their field of academic study. They are individuals who have mastered the art of learning content subjects and being graduate students they are aware of how to monitor and evaluate their subject knowledge and to find solutions to problems in their own research. These students should be trained to extend and apply such skills to the task of language learning through strategy training. Their experience with learning will make strategy training very challenging and motivating because it can result in their gaining greater control over their learning and their progress. The maturity of these graduate students makes them good candidates for strategy training (O'Malley & Chamot, 1990).

This also means that teachers will need to be adequately trained and prepared to conduct strategy training. This is because when teachers encourage independence and autonomy in learning, they must be prepared to give up some of the control that they had previously exercised. As Lynch notes, "Any move towards autonomy involves the realignment of traditional roles in language learning" (Lynch 2001:394).

I personally found that having this insight into the students' learning processes, achievements, frustrations, plans and preferences made me a more sensitive teacher as I responded to their needs. For example, through the learning diary I learned that a particularly critical student was actually reacting to the new learning environment he was now in. He harboured some misconceptions about his own level of proficiency and held negative ideas about some classroom activities. When the objectives for learning tasks were carefully explained to him and when he came to accept his true attainment level, he was more co-operative and more willing to participate in class.

It appears that giving learners strategy training and the opportunity and means for reflection can help some learners to understand more about their own language processes. In this study, this awareness and knowledge helped learners to better manage and direct their efforts and progress. The PRC learners in NUS have received strategy instruction positively and have used this new found knowledge to help them to better learn the English language. These results suggest that strategy training could be used by English language teachers in the PRC as they develop more learner-centred teaching methods and curricula that will suit their own culture and circumstance.

The goal of a language teacher is to see each student become an independent, self-directed, creative learner. With adequate strategy training this goal can be realised to the benefit of both teacher and student.

REFERENCES

Carter, R. (2001). Vocabulary. In R. Carter and D. Nunan (Eds.), *Teaching English to Speakers of Other Languages* (pp. 42–47). Cambridge: Cambridge University Press.

Chamot, A. U. (1987). The learning strategies of ESL students. In A. Wenden and J. Rubin (Eds.), *Learner Strategies in Language Learning* (pp. 71–83). Englewood Cliffs, NY: Prentice-Hall International.

_____ (1993). Student responses to learning strategy instruction in the foreign language classroom. *Foreign Language Annals,* 26(3): 308–321.

Cohen, A.D. & Aphek E. (1980). Retention of second language vocabulary over time: Investigating the role of mnemonic associations. *System,* 8: 221–35.

Cohen, A. D.; Weaver, S. J. & Li, T. Y. (1996). *The impact of strategies-based instruction speaking a foreign language.* Center for Advanced Research on Language Acquisition (CARLA). University of Minnesota Working Paper Series 4.

Lynch, T. (2001). Promoting EAP learner autonomy in a second language university context. In J. Flowerdew and M. Peacock (Eds.), *Research Perspectives on English for Academic Purposes* (pp. 390–403).Cambridge: Cambridge University Press.

McDonough, S.H. (1999). Learner strategies. *Language Teaching,* 32(1): 1–18.

Nunan, D. (1996). Learner strategy training in the classroom: An action research study. *TESOL Journal* 6(1): 35–41.

O'Malley, J. M. & Chamot A. U. (1990). *Learning Strategies in Second Language Acquisition.* Cambridge: Cambridge University Press.

O'Malley, J. M.; Chamot, A. U.; Stewner-Mazanares, G.; Russo, R. P. & Kupper, L. (1985). Learning strategy applications with students of English as a Second Language. *TESOL Quarterly,* 19(3): 557–84.

Oxford, R. L. (1990). *Language Learning Strategies: What Every Teacher Should Know.* NY: Newbury House Publishers.

_____ (2001). Language learning strategies. In R. Carter and D. Nunan (Eds.), *Teaching English to Speakers of Other Languages* (pp. 166–72). Cambridge: Cambridge University Press.

Rubin, J. (1975). What the "good language learner" can teach us. *TESOL* Quarterly, 9(1): 41–51.

_____ (1981). The study of cognitive processes in second language learning. *Applied Linguistics* 2: 117–31.

_____ (1987). Learner strategies: Theoretical assumptions, research history and typology. In A. Wenden and J. Rubin (Eds.), *Learner Strategies in Language Learning* (pp. 15–30). Englewood Cliffs. NY: Prentice-Hall International.

Rubin, J. & Thompson I. (1982). *How to Be a More Successful Language Learner.* Boston: Heinle & Heinle.

Stern, H. H. (1975). What can we learn from the good language learner? *Canadian Modern Language Review,* 3: 304–318.

Wenden, A. L. (1987). Conceptual background and utility. In A. Wenden and J. Rubin (Eds.), *Learner Strategies in Language Learning* (pp. 3–13). Englewood Cliffs, NY: Prentice-Hall International.

_____ (1991). *Learner Strategies for Learner Autonomy.* Englewood Cliffs, NY: Prentice-Hall International.

_____ (1996). Designing learner training: The curricular questions. In G. M. Jacobs (Ed.), *Language Classrooms of Tomorrow* (pp. 238–55). RELC Anthology Series 38. Singapore: SEAMEO Regional Language Centre.

APPENDIX A. FORMAT OF A LEARNING DIARY ENTRY

Date: _____

This week I studied :

This week I learned:

This week I used English in these places:

This week I spoke English with these people:

This week I made these mistakes:

My difficulties are:

I would like to know:

I would like help with:

My learning and practising goals for next week are:

CHAPTER 11

Language Learning Strategies and English Language Proficiency: An Investigation of Chinese ESL Students at NUS

ZHANG MINGYUAN [1] & LI XIAOPING

INTRODUCTION

Given the same learning environment, the same learning material, and the same teaching staff, ESL students vary greatly in the speed with which they learn the language (Ellis, 1997). Individual differences have been identified as variables influencing language learning outcomes (Altman, 1980; Skehan, 1989; Larsen-Freeman and Long, 1991). Of the individual differences identified, use of language learning strategy is a key factor affecting learners' rate of language acquisition and the ultimate level of language proficiency (Ellis, 1997).

Politzer and McGroarty (1985) examined the relationship between a range of 'good learning behaviours' by using a questionnaire and gain scores on an intensive course. They reported that certain individual strategies showed significant associations with their proficiency measures. They also found some differences in the reported strategy use between the two main groups, Asians and Hispanics. Green and Oxford (1995) reported that students who were better in their language performance generally reported higher levels of overall strategy use and frequent use of a greater number of strategy categories. McDonough (1999) pointed out that the strategies learners apply are sometimes not directly related to language learning but are characteristic features of

---

[1]The principal author collected the data while working at CELC (1998–2001).

the human brain. Grainger (1997) investigated the use of language learning strategies by learners of Japanese as a foreign language at a tertiary institution. A major finding was that students from European backgrounds and students from Asian backgrounds preferred different learning strategies.

However, there has been little study done on the relationship between Chinese ESL students' language learning strategies and their English proficiency. This study was therefore conducted to investigate the relationship between Chinese ESL learners' language learning strategies and their English proficiency so as to explore more effective means of English language teaching to Chinese ESL students.

Issues Related to Language Learning Strategies

To answer the question as to why some learners do better, researchers such as Rubin and Stern started researching on "what good learners can teach us?" (Rubin, 1975) and "what can we learn from good language learners?" (Stern, 1975). The studies started with the purpose of finding what successful students did and ended up forming the concept of learning strategies. Their studies have led to numerous investigations and discussions of the concept. The recognition of the existence of learning strategies has provided new insights for improving the efficiency and effectiveness of language learning and teaching.

There has been a great deal of debate on the appropriate way of defining language learning strategies. After reviewing the definitions of learning strategies by Chamot (1987), Oxford (1989), Rubin (1987), Stern (1983), and Weistein and Mayer (1986), Ellis (1997) defined language learning strategies as consisting of mental or behavioural activities related to some specific stage in the overall process of language acquisition or language use.

There are also many ways of classifying language learning strategies (Wong-Fillmore, 1976, 1979; Naiman et al., 1978; Rubin, 1981; Skehan, 1989). Two main ways of categorising learning strategies are reported here. The first was proposed by Oxford (1990). Oxford proposed six groups of strategies: (a) memory, (b) cognitive, (c) compensation, (d) metacognitive, (e) affective, and (f) social. The second was proposed by Chamot (1990). Chamot presented three major classes of strategies: (a) metacognitive, (b) cognitive, and (c) socio-affective.

Regardless of how language learning strategies are classified, research indicates that language learning may involve the use of several independent learning strategies that may have different effects on proficiency. Despite the problems in classifying strategies, researchers acknowledge that there are positive relationships between the frequent use of learning strategies and achievement in the language (Green and Oxford, 1995; Oxford and Burry-Stock, 1995; Oxford, Park-Oh, Ito and Sumrall, 1993).

RESEARCH DESIGN

Participants

The participants (98 male and 32 female) were all pre-matriculated students participating in a six-month intensive English programme at the National University of Singapore (NUS) before they became matriculated students at NUS' Faculty of Science and School of Computing. All participants, 18 years old on average, were from the People's Republic of China. They scored well in the National University Entrance Examination conducted by China's Ministry of Education and were all recruited by various universities in China. All participants had studied English as a subject for at least six years in junior and senior middle schools in China.

Instruments

The main instrument used in this study was the Strategy Inventory for Language Learning (SILL) developed by Oxford (1990). In the SILL, strategies are grouped into two types: direct (i.e., strategies which directly involve the target language) and indirect. The direct strategies include memory, cognitive, and compensation while the indirect ones include metacognitive, affective, and social.

Among direct strategies, memory strategies pertain to the storing and retrieval of information; for example, "I use new English words in a sentence so I can remember them." Cognitive strategies, although being controversial in their definitions, are about manipulation or transformation of the target language by the learner; for example,

"I use the English words I know in different ways." Compensation strategies help ESL learners to use the new language for either comprehension or production despite limitations in knowledge; for example, "To understand unfamiliar English words I make guesses."

Among indirect strategies, metacognitive strategies let learners control their own cognition; for example, "I look for people to talk to in English." Affective strategies relate to the regulation of feelings and attitudes; for example, "I try to relax whenever I feel afraid of using English." Social strategies are the ones that take account of the fact that language is a form of social behaviour, involving communication with other people, for example, "I practise English with other students."

Students in this study, according to the requirements of the SILL, responded to each item by circling on a 5-point Likert scale ranging from 1 ('Never or almost never true of me') to 5 ('Always or almost always true of me').

The other instrument, a proficiency test, was used to determine students' L2 proficiency in terms of vocabulary and grammar, composition, and oral communication. The same test was administered at the beginning and the end of the programme to collect two groups of data for comparison.

Procedures and Design

All participants took the English proficiency test as a pre-test at the first week of the programme. In the midst of the programme, students completed the SILL. At the end of the programme, they took the same proficiency test as a post-test.

In a study on the relationship between strategy use and language proficiency, Green and Oxford (1995) used proficiency as an independent variable and strategy use as a dependent variable. However, Bremner (1998) stated that if one assumes the goal of learning strategy research is to establish whether strategy use has a positive effect on the enhancement of proficiency, it would seem to be more logical to set strategy use as an independent variable.

In the current study, strategy use was used as an independent variable and proficiency as a dependent variable. The following questions were addressed:

1. How often do the Chinese students use different language learning strategies?
2. What is the relationship between the general use of language learning strategies and the overall increase of language proficiency?
3. What is the relationship between the use of specific language learning strategies and the sub skills of language proficiency?

FINDINGS

Application of All Language Learning Strategies

Students' responses to the questionnaire were computed to obtain the mean scores, representing the frequency of each strategy used by the students in this study. The calculated results indicate that the frequency the students used different strategies follows this order (from the highest to the lowest): compensation, metacognition, cognition, social factors, affective factors, and memory (see Figure 1). Compensation strategy (M=3.45) was most frequently used while memory strategy (M=2.93) was least frequently used.

Like the present study, Bremner (1998) used the SILL to survey the language learning strategies used by a group of Hong Kong learners. Table 1 is a comparison of Bremner's study and the present study. The results of both studies showed that compensation and metacognitive strategies were the most used, while affective and memory strategies were the least used. The only difference between the results of these

Table 1. A Comparison of the Results of Bremner's Study and the Present Study

Rank	This study	Bremner (1998)
1	Compensation (3.45)	Compensation (3.36)
2	Metacognitive (3.34)	Metacognitive (3.12)
3	Cognitive (3.13)	Cognitive (2.97)
4	Social (3.13)	Social (2.91)
5	Affective (2.96)	Affective (2.85)
6	Memory (2.93)	Memory (2.73)

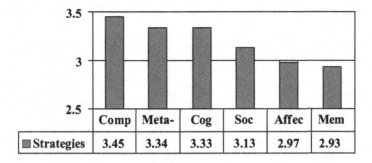

Figure 1.   Use of Language Learning Strategies

two studies is that the frequency of strategy use by the students in the present study is consistently higher than that of the study by the students in Bremner's study, though the differences did not seem to be significant. Considering the fact the students from both studies have Chinese as their mother tongue, the results from the present study and Bremner's appear to support the research findings by Politzer and McGroarty (1985) and Grainger (1997) that L2 learners from the same background tend to prefer the same language learning strategies.

Language Learning Strategies and Language Proficiency

In order to test the relationship between the overall increase in the language proficiency and the language learning strategy use as a whole, we divided our participants into three groups based on their use of all the strategies. Those using the least strategies were put into the low

Table 2. Analysis of Variance for Increase in Overall Proficiency by Overall Strategy Use

Source	D.F.	Sum of squares	Mean squares	F ratio	F prob.
Between Groups	2	362.9	181.5	3.62	.029
Within Groups	127	6365.4	50.1		
Total	129	6728.3			

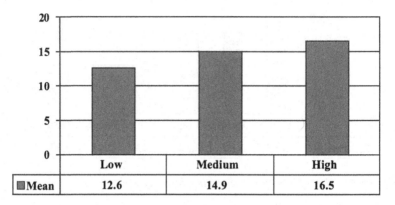

Figure 2.   Overall Increase in Proficiency by all Six Strategies

group, those using the medium strategies were put into the medium group, and those using the most strategies were put into the high group.

A one-way analysis of variance (ANOVA) statistical procedure was used to test the differences in the overall increase in language proficiency as a function of overall strategy use. As shown in Table 2, the analysis yielded a significant F ratio of 3.62, which indicated that there was a significant difference among the groups on the overall gain in language proficiency ($p < .029$). Follow-up analyses indicated that the high group (M=16.5) had a greater increase in proficiency than did the low group (M=12.6). The medium group had a mean of 14.9 (see Figure 2).

Language Proficiency and Metacognitive Strategy

In order to test the relationship between the overall increase in the language proficiency and the use of metacognitive strategy, we divided our participants into low, medium, and high groups according to their use of metacognitive strategies. One-way ANOVA was used to test the differences in the overall gain in language proficiency as a function of metacognitive strategy use. The analysis yielded a significant F ratio of 3.16, which indicated that there was a significant difference ($p < .05$) among the groups on the increased overall proficiency (Table 3). Follow-up analyses did not indicate any significant difference among the groups. The low group had a mean of 12.5, the medium group had a mean of

Table 3. Analysis of Variance for Increase in Overall Progress by Metacognitive Strategy Use

Source	D.F.	Sum of squares	Mean squares	F ratio	F prob.
Between Groups	2	319.02	159.51	3.16	.05
Within Groups	127	6409.31	50.47		
Total	129	6728.33			

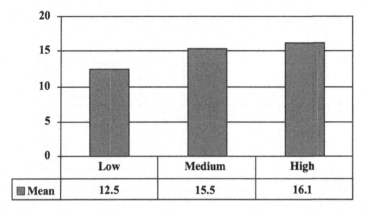

	Low	Medium	High
▨ Mean	12.5	15.5	16.1

Figure 3. Overall Increase in Proficiency by Metacognitive Strategy

15.5, and the high group had the mean of 16.1 (Figure 3). It seems that the more the students applied the metacognitive strategy the greater the overall increase they achieved between the pre-test and the post test.

Composition Proficiency and Memory Strategy

In order to test the relationship between the overall increase in the composition proficiency and the use of memory strategy, we divided our participants into three groups according to their use of memory strategies: a low group, a medium group, and a high group. The differences in the increase in composition proficiency as a function of memory strategy use was tested by one-way ANOVA. As shown in Table 4, the analysis yielded a significant *F* ratio of 3.35, which

Table 4. Analysis of Variance for Increase in Composition Proficiency by Memory Strategy Use

Source	D.F.	Sum of squares	Mean squares	F ratio	F prob.
Between Groups	2	476.99	238.49	3.35	.038
Within Groups	127	9034.40	71.14		
Total	129	9511.39			

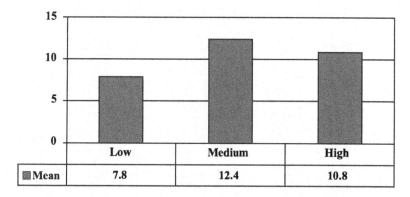

	Low	Medium	High
■Mean	7.8	12.4	10.8

Figure 4. Increase in Composition Proficiency by Use of Memory Strategy

indicated that there was a significant difference among the groups on the increased overall proficiency ($p < .038$). Follow-up analyses indicated that the medium group (M=12.4) had a greater increase in composition proficiency than the low group (M=7.8). The high group had a mean of 10.8 (Figure 4).

Oral Proficiency and Cognitive Strategy

In order to test the relationship between the overall increase in the oral English proficiency and the cognitive strategy use, we divided our participants into three groups based on their use of cognitive strategies: a low group, a medium group, and a high group. One-way ANOVA was used to test for differences in the increase in oral English proficiency

Table 5. Analysis of Variance for Increase in Oral English Scores by Cognitive Strategy

Source	D.F.	Sum of squares	Mean squares	F ratio	F prob.
Between Groups	2	469.1	234.5	5.1	.007
Within Groups	127	5746.4	45.2		
Total	129	6215.6			

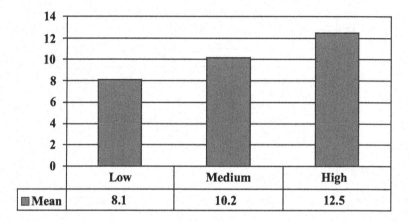

Figure 5.   Increase in Oral English by Use of Cognitive Strategy

as a function of cognitive strategy use. The *F* ratio was 5.1 (Table 5), indicating that the difference among the groups on the increase in oral English proficiency was significant (*p* < .007). Follow-up analyses indicated that the high group (M=12.5) had a significantly greater increase in oral English proficiency than did the low group (M=8.1). The medium group had a mean of 10.2.

Composition Proficiency and Affective Strategy

In order to test the relationship between the overall increase in the composition proficiency and the affective strategy use, we divided our participants into three groups according to their use of affective

Table 6. Analysis of Variance for Increase in Composition Scores by Affective Strategies

Source	D.F.	Sum of squares	Mean squares	F ratio	F prob.
Between Groups	2	455.7	227.8	3.19	.04
Within Groups	127	9055.7	71.3		
Total	129	9511.4			

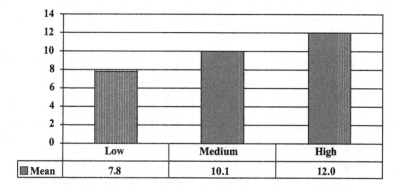

	Low	Medium	High
☐ Mean	7.8	10.1	12.0

Figure 6.   Increase in Composition Proficiency by Use of Affective Strategy

strategies: a low group, a medium group, and a high group. One-way analysis of variance statistical procedure was used to test for differences in the increase of composition proficiency as a function of affective strategy use. As shown in Table 6, the *F* ratio of 3.19, indicated that there was a significant difference among the groups on the increase in composition proficiency ($p < .04$). Follow-up analyses indicated that the high group (M=12.0) had a greater increase in composition proficiency than the medium group (M=10.1). The low group had a mean of 7.8 (Figure 6).

DISCUSSION

In this section, the findings of the study will be discussed first, and then implications of the study drawn. The major purpose of this investigation was to determine the relationship between the use of language learning strategies and gain in English proficiency.

General Use of Language Learning Strategies

The present study found that PRC students used compensation strategies most, followed by metacognitive strategies, cognitive strategies, social strategies, affective strategies, and memory strategies. Using the same instrument, Bremner (1998) surveyed the language learning strategies used by a group of Hong Kong learners and came to a similar conclusion that compensation and metacognitive strategies were the most used and affective and memory strategies were the least used. The finding from the present study also reinforces the findings by Grainger (1997) and by Politzer and McGroarty (1985) that students from the same backgrounds tend to prefer the same strategies.

This finding and findings from similar studies have pedagogical implications. One such implication is that when ESL teachers provide learning strategies to their students, particularly students from the same background, they should be aware that the students tend to prefer identical strategies. Therefore the teachers should pay more attention to those strategies that are less frequently used. This can be done by drawing students' attention to such strategies and getting them to apply them in language learning.

Language Proficiency and Use of Six Strategies

When all six categories were combined and used as an independent variable, the results indicated that the more students used all the strategies, the more progress they made in their language proficiency. This finding shows that the general level of use of language strategies is a significant predictor for students' progress in this intensive English programme.

Language Proficiency and Metacognitive Strategy

When metacognitive strategy was used as an independent variable, the result indicated that the more the students used this particular strategy, the more progress they made in their overall language proficiency. This finding supported the belief by O'Malley and Chamot (1990) that "not all strategies are equivalent". Metacognitive strategy, which includes goal setting, planning, monitoring, and evaluating, is one of the most effective language learning strategies. When designing a training programme on using language learning strategies, educators may like to focus on metacognitive strategy use.

Composition Proficiency and Memory and Affective Strategies

When memory and affective strategies were used as individual variables respectively, they both showed significant impact on the progress students made in writing compositions. It indicates that training on how to use memory and affective strategies might increase students' progress in composition since memory strategy will enhance students' use of authentic language rather than creating non-standard English or 'Chinglish' and the use of affective strategy makes students feel less ill-at-ease, more confident and self-assured when writing.

Oral Proficiency and Cognitive Strategy

When cognitive strategy was used as an independent variable, the finding indicated that the more students used this strategy, the more progress they made in their proficiency in oral English. This finding shows that the use of cognitive strategies is a significant indicator of student's progress in oral English in this intensive English programme. Since cognitive strategy is more concerned with the direct activities that promote learning, the strategy represents what students actually do in oral communication. This is also different from indirect strategies that have more to do with affective feelings.

The results of this study indicated a relationship between the use of language learning strategies and English proficiency. However, the relationship between the use of language learning strategies and English proficiency in this study should be interpreted with caution. One obvious question is whether such findings should be interpreted as being a correlational or causal relationship.

INTERPRETATION OF FINDINGS

There are three possible ways of looking at strategies and their relationship with proficiency. The first is to see the use of strategies as an outcome of proficiency and this being the case there is no necessity to further investigate them, but to focus on what helps students acquire proficiency. The second is to see them as having a uni-directional causal role in increasing proficiency, but there is no strong evidence for this as yet. The third is to accept the view of McIntyre (1994), and Green and Oxford (1995) that relationship between the two is mutual, and that causality is bi-directional.

Green and Oxford (1995), in examining the relationship between proficiency and language learning strategy use, reported "students who were better in their language performance generally reported higher levels of overall strategy use and greater use of a greater number of strategy categories" (p. 265). Regarding the association between reported strategy use and proficiency, particularly the issue of causality, Skehan (1989) and Rees-Miller (1993) pointed out that the existence of causality is a subject of debate and the correlation between the two may not necessarily suggest the causality in a particular direction. When reporting that more proficient students make better use of strategies, McIntyre's interpretation is that "either proficiency influences the choice of strategies or that strategy choice is simply a sign of proficiency level" (p. 188).

Our interpretation is that there is a causality relationship between proficiency and strategy use. It might not be a one-way causality. To be more exact, it is an interactive causality relationship. While active use of strategies helps students attain higher proficiency, the high proficiency, in turn, makes it more likely that students will select more active use of strategies.

RECOMMENDATIONS FOR ESL TEACHERS

As is indicated in this study, there is a strong relationship between the use of language learning strategies and language proficiency. However, if we accept the assumption that strategy use and language proficiency are mutual and bi-directional, we might draw some pedagogical implications. Park (1997) reported a significant relationship between language learning strategies and Test of English as a Foreign Language (TOEFL) scores and also found that all six categories of language learning strategies were correlated with TOEFL scores. He suggested that strategy training should be conducted in classrooms to help students become autonomous L2 learners outside the classrooms where much L2 learning occurs. Therefore, one way to increase the Chinese students' language proficiency is to provide training on the use of language learning strategies.

Three different methods for training the Chinese students' use of language strategies are introduced below.

Training on Raising Awareness of Learning Strategies

This training is for the purpose of raising learners' consciousness of the existence of the language strategies. Participants become aware of and familiar with the general idea of language learning strategies. They are exposed to situations where strategies are applied in helping L2 learners solve a variety of language tasks. In this training, however, the students actually do not engage themselves in any application of language learning strategies.

The training on raising the awareness is an important step leading students to becoming conscious users of various strategies. Probably, it is often the first time these Chinese students are acquainted with the concept of learning strategies. Therefore, its introduction and instruction should be fun and motivating so that participants will be encouraged to construct and expand their knowledge of strategies at a later time. For this reason, it is best not to use a lecture format for this training.

Intensive Language Learning Strategy Training

Intensive language learning strategy training is best conducted in a workshop format where students will be involved in learning and practising of a number of strategies that are suitable for the particular language level of the students. The teaching should be done with actual learning tasks, usually those found in the language learning programmes. The advantage of this training is that the teacher has total control of time and students will get intensive training and be able to associate the strategies with their learning at hand immediately. The disadvantage is that the workshop might not have adequate long-term effect on enhancing students' use of the learning strategies due to the time constraints of what can be covered in a short time.

Strategy Training Incorporated into Regular Teaching

The incorporated training is probably the most effective of all training methods mentioned here. This method, like the intensive strategy training, involves learning and practising with actual language tasks. The main difference is the time: it is not a one-time workshop. The training is incorporated into the learning and teaching activities.

Sometimes, however, students might have a feeling that this approach appears to be haphazard because, due to the constraints of the teaching material, the teacher might not be able to introduce and provide training in all strategies systematically. To solve this problem, the teacher needs to design activities and choose appropriate material to introduce and provide training in all learning strategies systematically. This approach may leave a deeper impression on students and should work well with most students due to the consistency and wide coverage of the strategies.

Whichever type of training a teacher chooses, a practical procedure will usually consist of four steps. Here is a description of these four steps.

(1) *Determine the needs.* The teacher should assess what needs there are. To begin with the teacher can introduce some real examples L2 learners face in their learning and ask students how they will solve them. Then the teacher can show the students how the problems could be solved by applying certain types of strategy. Students might develop a great interest in such strategies and will most likely ask for training on language learning strategies.

(2) *Select a strategy or strategies.* The choice of strategies should depend largely on the ESL students' language proficiency or the emphasis of the course (oral or written communication). Those strategies that are easy to apply, for example, direct strategies which directly involve the target language, can be taught first. Difficult ones, such as indirect strategies, will be introduced later.

(3) *Prepare teaching material and learning activities.* This is a key step that will lead to the success of the training. Careful planning have to be made. Sometimes a well-planned activity might not work as well as expected, but teachers will gradually build up their expertise and will be able to train the students more successfully.

(4) *Conduct and evaluate the training.* Students will be given plenty of opportunities to practise the strategies being taught. Teachers' evaluation and reflection on implementation of various strategies are crucial. The evaluation needs to be carried out at different steps of the planning and training process. This will enable further modification for future instruction.

CONCLUSION

Despite the problems in defining and classifying language learning strategies, research continues to support the theory that learning strategies help learners take control of their learning and become more proficient learners. The findings from the present study confirm the conclusions by other researchers (Green and Oxford, 1995; McIntyre, 1994) that language learning strategies are related to language proficiency and that the use of different strategies might lead to an improvement in different areas of language development.

The findings from the present study seem to support the suggestion by other researchers (McIntyre, 1994; Skehan, 1989; and Rees-Miller, 1993) that there is a relationship between proficiency and strategy use. However, the general disposition is that such a relationship is not a one-way but rather an interactive relationship. While active use of strategies helps students attain higher proficiency, the high proficiency, in turn, makes students more active users of different strategies. Therefore, language teachers should not only depend on teaching language *per se* but also engage students in a variety of activities by various methods to make students better and more autonomous language learners. Training on strategy use may be one of the answers.

REFERENCES

Altman, H. (1980). Foreign language teaching: focus on the learner. In H. Altman & C. V. James (Eds.), *Foreign Language Teaching: Meeting Individual Needs* (pp. 30–45). Oxford: Pergamon.

Bremner, S. (1998). Language learning strategies and language proficiency: Investigating the relationship in Hong Kong. *Canadian Modern Language Review*, 55(4): 490–514.

Chamot, A. (1987). The learning strategies of ESL students. In A. Wenden & J. Rubin (Eds.), *Learner Strategies in Language Learning* (pp. 108–125). Englewood Cliffs, NJ: Prentice Hall.

_____ (1990). Cognitive instruction in the second language classroom: The role of learning strategies. *Georgetown University Round Table on Languages and Linguistics*, pp. 496–513.

Ellis, R. (1997). *The Study of Second Language Acquisition*. Oxford: Oxford University Press.

Grainger, P. (1997). Language-learning strategies for learners of Japanese: Investigating ethnicity. *Foreign Language Annals*, 30: 378–85.

Green, J. M. & Oxford, R. L. (1995). A closer look at learning strategies, L2 proficiency, and gender. *TESOL Quarterly*, 29: 261–97.

Larsen-Freeman, D. & Long, M. (1991). *An Introduction to Second Language Acquisition Research*. London: Longman.

McDonough, S. H. (1999). Learner Strategies. *Language Teaching*, 32: 1–18.

McIntyre, P. D. (1994). Toward a social psychological model of strategy use. *Foreign Language Annuals*, 27: 185–95.

Naiman, N.; Frohlich, M.; Stern, H. & Todesco, A. (1978). *The Good Language Learner*. Research in Education Series, No. 7. Toronto: The Ontario Institute for Studies in Education.

O'Malley, J. M. & Chamot, A. U. (1990). *Learning Strategies and Second Language Acquisition*. Cambridge: Cambridge University Press.

Oxford, R. (1989). Use of language learning strategies: a synthesis of studies with implications for teacher training. *System*, 17: 235–47.

_____ (1990). *Language Learning Strategies: What every teacher should know*. Boston: Heinle & Heinle Publishers.

Oxford, R. L. & Burry-Stock, J. (1995). Assessing the use of language learning strategies worldwide with the ESL/EFL version with the strategy inventory of language learning (SILL). *System*, 23: 1–23.

Oxford, R. L.; Park-Oh, Y.; Ito, S. & Sumrall, M. (1993). Japanese by satellite: Effects of motivation, language learning styles and strategies, gender, course level, and previous language learning experience on Japanese language achievement. *Foreign Language Annals*, 26: 359–71.

Park, G. (1997). Language learning strategies and English proficiency in Korean university students. *Foreign Language Annals*, 30: 211–21.

Politzer, R.L. & McGroarty, M. (1985). An exploratory study of learning behaviours and their relationship to gains in linguistic and communicative competence. *TESOL Quarterly*, 19: 103–123.

Rees-Miller, J. (1993). A critical appraisal of learner training: Theoretical bases and teaching implications. *TESOL Quarterly*, 27: 679–89.

Rubin, J. (1975). What the 'good language learner' can teach us. *TESOL Quarterly*, 9: 41–51.

_____ (1981). Study of cognitive processes in second language learning. *Applied Linguistics*, 11: 117–31.

_____ (1987). Learner strategies: Theoretical assumptions, research history and typology. In A. Wenden & J. Rubin (Eds.), *Learner Strategies in Language Learning* (pp. 133–44). Englewood Cliffs, NJ: Prentice Hall.

Skehan, P. (1989). *Individual Differences in Second-language Learning*. London: Edward Arnold.

Stern, H. H. (1975). What can we learn from the good language learner? *The Canadian Modern Language Review*, 31: 304–318.

_____ (1983). *Fundamental Concepts of Language Teaching*. Oxford: Oxford University Press.

Weinstein, C. & Mayer, R. (1986). The teaching of learning strategies. In M. Wittrock (Ed.), *Handbook of Research on Teaching* (pp. 315–27). New York: Macmillan.

Wong-Fillmore, L. (1976). The second time around: Cognitive and social strategies in second language acquisition. Unpublished PhD thesis, Stanford University.

_____ (1979). Individual differences in second language acquisition. In C. J. Fillmore; D. Kempler & W. S. Y. Wang (Eds.), *Individual Differences in Language Ability and Language Behavior* (pp. 203–228). New York: Academic Press.